RICK STEIN'S
Food Stories

RICK STEIN'S
Food Stories

BBC
BOOKS

CONTENTS

Argyll and Bute has always been a mystical and magical place for me ever since I first went there with my parents as a twelve-year-old and stayed in the Crinan Hotel. The area is made up of fingers of land with water in between, the longest finger being the Kintyre peninsula. It's so close to Glasgow as the crow flies, but so far unless you take the ferry to get there. It seems to me that tourists drive north from Glasgow, skirting Loch Lomond and then keep on towards Fort William and the Highlands, not thinking to turn left and back south to Lochgilphead and down to Loch Fyne. On the eastern shore of this beautiful stretch of water is an isolated restaurant called Inver, a converted croft and a collection of low white bothies with serene views across the cold waters of the loch. There's a ruined fifteenth-century castle on a promontory of rock nearby and beyond, thirty miles of the peninsula ending at the Mull of Kintyre. A breathtaking scene and I recalled the words in Paul McCartney's song: 'My desire is always to be here'. No wonder, I thought at the time.

I was there filming an episode for my series *Food Stories* and went foraging for sea herbs with Pam Brunton who, with her partner Rob, runs Inver and cooks exquisite dishes, all local and featuring Herdwick lamb from the Isle of Bute, langoustines, lobsters and hand-dived scallops and oysters from the loch, and bass, halibut and turbot from the sea around the isles of Islay, Mull and Arran. It was May and I was freezing as I only had on a thin summer jacket. 'Ne'er cast a clout till May is out', as the locals say.

We gathered sea broccoli, sweet cicely, cuckoo flower and scurvy grass – which tasted hotter than horseradish – to adorn many of Pam's dishes, such as the honey-glazed, barbecued neck of lamb with creamed cannellini beans she cooked for me. The recipe for her beans is on page 259, but sadly the lamb needed Pam's restaurant kitchen techniques and could not be simplified for cooking at home without becoming a pale imitation. Everything about Pam was admirable: a bundle of energy with a sweet smile and an intelligent and practical take on the common sense of keeping all her dishes local. 'Why would you not?' she says. 'My suppliers are my friends and, a lot of the time, my customers'.

That trip to Argyll was something I will never forget. I'm sure it's a part of the country that many of us don't visit but anyone who does will be overwhelmed by how beautiful and relatively unspoiled it is. To me, it's a bit like the Isle of Wight in that it seems like a step back in time. I often say that as much as I love making television series it's when I go back somewhere on holiday that I really appreciate places. I will hasten back to Inver with its wooden floors and rugs, log fires and warm dishes of local food.

I met so many dedicated people like Pam and Rob when filming *Food Stories*, but the series and this book are not only about celebrating the great food we have in the UK. They are also about what we love to eat now. And this is underlined by the fact that we live in one of the most multicultural places in the world as far as food is concerned. I was initially inspired by a very influential cookery book called *It's All American Food* by David Rosengarten which was first published in 2003. It has the simple premise that classic American dishes like meatloaf, clam chowder and Thanksgiving turkey are all very fine but really American food is what Americans like to eat today, dishes that come from the vast array of immigrant communities who've arrived there in the last couple of hundred years from almost every country in the world – China, Poland, Germany, Italy and so on.

Much the same can be said about the United Kingdom, but this is not the case in countries like Italy, France and Spain. I think the reason for this is that our Industrial Revolution, which happened much earlier in the UK than in other countries, disconnected so much of the population from their local cuisine. This was followed by a demand for cheap labour from countries such as the Indian subcontinent and China, and those people brought their cooking traditions with them. In most of Europe, in contrast, people stayed much more attached to the land and therefore their food remained more traditionally based. Of course, things have changed a great deal. You can now get almost as wide a variety of cuisines in Paris as in London – but not quite. And thanks to some particular links to countries like India through colonial expansion the UK does have some of the best Indian restaurants in the world.

Our country is now an amazingly fertile place for food stories, not only because of the immigration histories of the Italians in Glasgow, Chinese in Liverpool and London, even Koreans in New Malden and Nepalese in Kent to name a few, but also the many enterprising entrepreneurial activities. For instance, at Bundobust in Leeds, we discovered Lithuanian brewers teaming up with Gujarati vegetarian cooks to produce a revolution in traditional Indian restaurants.

Both the restaurant staff and brewers at Bundobust were young and one of the pleasures of filming the *Food Stories* series was seeing the energy and hope of the twenty- and thirty-year-olds involved in

'It seems to
me that great
food crosses
boundaries
and brings
people together
so naturally.'

food. I'm thinking in particular of a couple of young chocolatiers I met in an area of Glasgow called Merchant City, which is full of enterprising small businesses. Cameron and Lara run Bare Bones. They import raw cacao beans from different small cooperatives around the world, all with their own characteristics and flavour, to make their chocolate. With their enthusiasm and keen understanding of 'terroir', they reminded me of young winemakers. They have developed their own process in which the beans are roasted, then stone-ground with sugar for three days and when I tasted the results it was a revelation. You could identify so many different flavours. When I told them it was the best chocolate I'd ever tasted I meant it.

Then there was the surprise of tasting my first-ever Filipino dish in Belfast! It was a cold drizzly Sunday in May when I visited a market where the stalls were made entirely from shipping containers on the site of a demolished cinema. I have to say that at the time I didn't expect this to be a great day's filming, but as soon as I started talking to Nallaine, owner of a little food stall called Kubo and who was so full of humour and enthusiasm for her country's cuisine, I realised this was going to be a perfect story about food from the other side of the world being brought to the UK. She produced the Filipino version of Sunday lunch which involved seven or eight classic Filipino dishes, the most memorable of which for me was a pork belly adobo – you'll find my version of her recipe on page 179. Traditionally, all the food is eaten with your fingers – something I find particularly difficult even though I've had similar teaching in India – but Nallaine showed me what to do. Even with the slight pressure of television cameras on us all I was filled with a joy of digging in and sharing in that very informal way. Half the other people at that lunch were from Northern Ireland, not the Philippines, but all were loving what they were eating. It seems to me, as I'm afraid I keep reiterating, that great food crosses boundaries and brings people together so naturally.

As another example of how quickly our own country has assimilated tastes from afar, we went to film at a tofu factory just outside Leeds. I have to report with some humour, that health and safety requirements, now so common throughout the UK, required us to attend a short lecture before we donned our white coats and hats, beard guards and plastic galoshes. This last bit of kit meant that we were told to hold on to the railings of metal stairs in the factory! However, it was fascinating to see really good-quality tofu produced by a Yorkshire team. Making tofu is a bit like making cheese and what

I particularly liked here was the way the tofu was hand cut, giving it a pleasingly artisan look. It also tasted really wonderful and gave us all a great desire to eat it. I have to say I'm very happy with my recipe for pad Thai noodles with tofu on page 108.

Another element of *Food Stories* echoes a series I made more than twenty years ago called *Food Heroes*, in which I looked at the efforts of people such as farmers, bakers, cheesemakers and fishermen who work so hard to provide us with amazing food. My admiration for fishermen in particular is unabated. When filming, I went out from Ramsgate in Kent with a young fisherman called Tom Bennet to catch Dover soles, a prime example of great British produce. As I said at the time, these are probably my favourite fish. They combine a satisfyingly firm texture and sweetness with the additional advantage of the easy way the fillets lift away from the bone, making them a joy to eat. As ever, I find myself challenged by the paradox of a working life that is so hard but carried out with such evident pleasure and satisfaction. Fishermen just love being out there.

Warming to the subject of food heroes, I felt that I absolutely had to visit a famous West Country organic vegetable grower called Guy Singh-Watson at Riverford Farm in Devon. I reminded him that when I first visited years ago, he was operating almost like a farm stall with an honesty box, and he admitted he started selling veg out of the back of his car. He now runs a business with a turnover of over a £100 million and he's stuck to his principles – no pesticides, fertilisers or indeed any chemicals. Instead, he works in harmony with nature: for example, introducing insects into his greenhouses to kill pests. Guy pioneered the whole idea of veg boxes and now delivers to more than 200,000 homes all around the country. Having left Riverford with a bag full of multi-coloured beets and carrots, I was more than happy to go vegetarian for a day and made a vegetable tarte tatin, which you will find on page 95.

Finally, my other mission was to take a look at what are now the nation's favourite dishes. Post-war, these would mostly have been meat and two veg recipes. I asked Portia Spooner, who's been massively helpful in testing dishes and coming up with ideas, not only to go online to look at charts and polls about what people are eating but also to visit loads of supermarkets and see what is being offered in the ever-expanding ready meal ranges and investigate what they now sell in their international sections. Many of the recipes in the book have come as a result of this research. Obvious examples are lasagne, chicken tikka masala and burritos, but there are also recipes for Korean fried chicken, Chinese bao buns and Thai curries.

So here it is. Not only a collection of the dishes that we, as a nation, like to eat now but also some new versions of my own favourites which are also loved by everyone else, such as roast beef, fish pie, grilled fish, fruit crumble and trifle. Food is obviously important to us – we have to eat to live, after all – but it is also an unusual and incredibly important way of understanding who we are as a nation. It tells a story about us and brings people together. It's really why I love doing what I do: when you're talking food to anybody it's always a pleasure. And that is because for most of the people involved in food in any way it's also a passion and that is something I find all over the UK.

I find it extraordinary that there are still French people who have never been to this country but think that all our food is about boiled meat and overcooked cabbage. How wrong they are. The UK is such a great country to eat in now and I hope you will join me in cooking and enjoying the dishes in this book.

STARTERS & LIGHT MEALS

Sas and I had a great dinner at the Devonshire in Soho recently. It's very well known for its beef cooked over hot coals and they serve endless pints of Guinness, but what I particularly liked was the procession of tapas-style dishes they brought to us beforehand, with some large, just-baked dinner rolls which you tear apart to eat with the food and soak up the juices. I've noticed that the concept of a large board of what I would call nibbles has taken off all over the place, both in the UK and in Australia. I guess it's a change from traditional first courses – just have a look at Pinterest and you'll see what I mean. I can see how this allows for conversation and conviviality while having a few bites at the same time. You'll find my suggestion for a sharing board and a recipe for dinner rolls in this chapter, and I've also included some other ideas for popular starters, ranging from a simple leek and potato soup to my take on a prawn cocktail. Many of these dishes are also just right for a snack or light lunch – for instance, the seared tuna salad or the peach and mozzarella salad make a welcome meal at any time of day.

Fresh spring rolls, also known as summer rolls, are all about contrasts of texture and fresh flavours. The rice paper wrappers are so thin that you can see the colours and shapes of the vegetable and prawn filling inside. I always think that spring rolls must be accompanied by a dipping sauce with the essential flavour groups – salty, sweet, sour and spicy.

VIETNAMESE FRESH SPRING ROLLS MAKES 8

35g rice vermicelli noodles
16 chives
8 coriander sprigs
1 carrot, grated or cut
    into matchsticks
¼ cucumber, deseeded
    and cut into matchsticks
50g fresh bean sprouts
½ little gem lettuce,
    finely shredded
125g cooked, peeled prawns,
    halved lengthways
1–2 tbsp roasted peanuts,
    roughly chopped (optional)
16 mint leaves
8 rice paper wrappers

Chilli dipping sauce
2 tbsp lime juice
2 tbsp fish sauce
1 tbsp sugar
1 tsp freshly grated
    root ginger
1 red bird's-eye chilli,
    thinly sliced
1 garlic clove, grated

Start with the vermicelli noodles. Bring a pan of water to the boil, drop in the noodles, then take the pan off the heat. Leave the noodles to soak for 2 minutes, then drain and rinse them under cold water. Drain well and set aside.

Mix all the chilli dipping sauce ingredients together in a bowl with 2 tablespoons of cold water and set aside.

Have all the filling ingredients prepared and close to hand. Dip a rice paper wrapper in a bowl of cold water and leave it to soak for up to a minute, then transfer it to a damp tea towel.

Being careful not to overfill and leaving a border around the edge to seal the roll, add the filling ingredients as follows: arrange 2 chives in an X pattern in the middle, add a sprig of coriander, then some noodles, carrot, cucumber, bean sprouts, lettuce, prawns and peanuts, if using. Top with a couple of mint leaves.

Fold the edge nearest you over the filling, tuck the sides over to enclose the ends, then roll away from you to seal in the filling. Set aside under a folded damp tea towel to prevent the roll drying out. Repeat with the remaining rice papers and filling. Serve with individual bowls of dipping sauce.

I guess the reason our native brown shrimps are not more acclaimed than they are is just that they're so tiny, because the flavour of them is superb. I wrote this recipe after a trip to Morecambe Bay where I watched the dredged shrimps being landed and then went to Ray Edmondson's little fish shop where he boils them and pots them in spiced butter. Normally, I just like to eat potted shrimps cold or warmed through with toast, but they are such a delicacy that I thought I'd make them into a rather special dish with some British crumpets and poached eggs. You'll find that home-made crumpets look more like muffins than the commercial versions, but what I love is that the melted spiced butter seeps into the holes in the crumpets.

CRUMPETS WITH POTTED SHRIMPS & POACHED EGGS SERVES 6

Potted shrimps
100g butter
2 blades of mace
Large pinch of cayenne pepper
Large pinch of ground
    white pepper
300g cooked, peeled
    brown shrimps
6 tbsp clarified butter
    (see p.270)

Crumpets
150g plain flour
1 tsp fast-action dried yeast
½ tsp salt
½ tsp sugar
1 tsp baking powder
200ml lukewarm water
30g unsalted butter, melted,
    plus soft butter for greasing

To serve
6 eggs, for poaching
A few chives, snipped

For the shrimps, put the butter in a pan with the mace, cayenne and white pepper and melt over a low heat to infuse the butter with the spices. Add the peeled shrimps and heat them through for a few minutes, but don't allow the mixture to boil. Divide the prawns between 6 ramekins and spoon a tablespoon of clarified butter into each. Leave to cool and set before serving.

To make the crumpets, mix the flour, yeast, salt, sugar and baking powder in a large bowl. Add the water and beat with an electric whisk for a few minutes until well combined. Cover the bowl with cling film and leave in a warm place for 30 minutes or until the mixture is bubbly on the surface and slightly increased in volume.

Grease 6 crumpet rings with butter. Brush a non-stick frying pan with half the melted butter and heat over a medium-high heat. Place 3 of the rings in the pan and pour one-sixth of the mixture into each ring. Cook for a couple of minutes, then reduce the heat to medium and cook for a further 4–5 minutes, until the surface of each crumpet is full of holes and looks fairly dry.

Carefully remove the rings, using a palette knife if required, then flip the crumpets over and cook for about 30 seconds to allow them to take on a little colour. Repeat with the remaining mixture. Cool on a wire rack or serve immediately while warm. If not using the crumpets immediately, toast them before serving.

Poach the eggs. Serve each crumpet with a poached egg and some potted shrimps, then garnish with snipped chives.

There's an amusing Australian phrase for complex recipes: project cooking. Maybe this applies to sushi, but they're easier to make than you think, thanks to nori mats and a little clear plastic device I've discovered recently for moulding the nigiri. Armed with these – and if you oil your hands when moulding the rice for the nigiri – you should be fine. You'll find making sushi very satisfying.

SEA BASS, CRAB MEAT & AVOCADO SUSHI

**MAKES ABOUT 16 MAKI AND 8 NIGIRI SUSHI
ENOUGH FOR 2–3 PEOPLE, MORE IF SERVING WITH DRINKS**

Sushi rice
300g sushi rice
60ml rice vinegar
1 tbsp caster sugar
¾ tsp salt

Nigiri
120g fresh (sushi-grade) sea
    bass or sea bream fillet
Wasabi
Soy sauce

Maki rolls
2 sheets of nori seaweed,
    cut in half
100g cooked white crab meat
1 tbsp mayonnaise (preferably
    Kewpie Japanese mayo)
1 small avocado, sliced

To serve
Soy sauce
Wasabi
Pickled ginger

Wash the rice 4 or 5 times in a bowl of cold water, stirring with each water change until the water runs clear. Cover the rice with plenty of cold water and leave to soak for 30 minutes. Drain the rice and add it to a pan with 390ml of water. Cover the pan and bring the water to the boil, then turn down the heat and cook very gently for 10–12 minutes until the water has been absorbed. Take the pan off the heat, set it aside with the lid on and leave the rice to steam for a further 10–15 minutes.

Mix the rice vinegar, sugar and salt and stir into the rice while it's still hot, making sure the mixture is well distributed. Tip the rice on to a large plate or tray, cover with a clean tea towel and allow to cool.

Nigiri: Skin the fish and slice it on the diagonal into 8 pieces about the size of your thumb. Using oiled hands and a nigiri mould, if you have one, shape some rice into 8 lozenges 5–6cm long. Smear the top of each with a little wasabi, then top with a slice of fish. Brush the top of the fish with soy sauce, then serve with more soy sauce, wasabi and pickled ginger.

Maki rolls: Arrange a half nori sheet on a sushi mat and spread it with a layer of rice, leaving a border of about 1cm on the edge furthest from you. Make a slight indent across the rice about halfway up. Mix the crab and mayo together and arrange a quarter of this along the indent, then add a couple of slices of avocado.

Using the mat, roll away from you, catching the filling into the roll. Continue with the remaining ingredients to make 3 more rolls. Using a wet knife blade or a serrated bread knife, cut each roll into 4 slices. Clean the knife blade between cuts to ensure a clean edge. Serve with soy sauce, wasabi and pickled ginger.

I note that there are now whole books devoted to cooking with air fryers. I wasn't sure about them at first, but I've realised that this is a perfect recipe to make in an air fryer or a frying pan.

HALLOUMI FRIES WITH A RED PEPPER DIP **SERVES 4–6**

2 x 225g blocks of
   halloumi cheese
4 tbsp plain flour
1 heaped tsp smoked sweet
   paprika (pimentón)
1–2 medium eggs, beaten
   (start with 1 and use
   a second if required)
100g panko breadcrumbs
Olive oil or sunflower oil,
   for frying

Dipping sauce
200g roasted red peppers
   (from a jar)
1 tbsp sriracha sauce

For the dipping sauce, combine the red peppers and sriracha in a blender and whizz until smooth. Scoop into a bowl and set aside.

Cut the halloumi into batons. You should get 10–12 from each block. Mix together the plain flour and paprika. Dip the halloumi batons into the flour mixture, then into the beaten egg and lastly the panko crumbs. Set them aside on a tray.

Heat a few tablespoons of oil in a frying pan and fry the breaded halloumi fries in batches until golden. When all the fries are cooked, serve immediately with the red pepper dip.

Alternatively, you can cook the halloumi fries in an air fryer. Spray the coated halloumi with olive oil and space them out so that they are not touching. Cook for about 8 minutes at 200°C, turning them halfway through.

Leek and potato soup is as much a part of our cuisine as it is of France. My early memories of this comforting first course are from table d'hôte fixed price menus during trips to France in the sixties – the soup always being served with lots of black pepper. I have to say that I don't think this is a soup that fares well with vegetable stock; it really should be made with good chicken stock.

LEEK, POTATO & THYME SOUP SERVES 4

500g leeks
30g butter
350g floury potatoes,
    peeled and cut into
    rough 3cm chunks
1 litre good chicken stock
Couple of thyme sprigs, leaves
    stripped from the stalks
200ml double cream, plus
    extra to serve if desired
1 tbsp chopped parsley
Salt and black pepper

Trim the leeks and cut them in half lengthways. Slice them and wash them really well to get rid of any grit and soil, then drain in a colander.

Heat the butter in a large pan. Add the leeks and potatoes and cook over a medium heat for 10–15 minutes until starting to soften, then add the chicken stock and thyme. Season with salt and black pepper, bring to the boil, then turn down the heat and leave to simmer for about 20 minutes.

Once the potatoes and leeks are really tender, blend the soup with a stick blender or liquidiser until smooth. Stir in the cream, then bring the soup back up to a simmer and check the seasoning – I like plenty of black pepper.

Serve in warm bowls and swirl in a little extra cream, if you like. Sprinkle with some chopped parsley.

My reason for including this recipe in the book is that apart from the fact that it's the first dish I ever ate at a Chinese restaurant – in Peterborough, in 1964 as it happens – it's also a world classic but is so often ruined by tasteless crab and gloopy cornflour. I thought it would be interesting to restore the dish to its simplicity and reliance on good fresh ingredients. Paradoxically, when you first taste it you'll probably find it a bit under-flavoured, but I hope its subtlety will appeal to you. The one ingredient missing is MSG. It's now understood that MSG is not an instigator of headaches, trembling, sweating and whatever else has been ascribed to it. It's about as dangerous as salt and is mostly produced by bacterial fermentation like vinegar. I've never owned up to having a tub of Aromat in my store cupboard, but I've always had one and can now admit to sprinkling it on my crab and sweetcorn soup. The choice is yours.

CRAB & SWEETCORN SOUP SERVES 4

Stock
1.2 litres good chicken stock
6 thin slices of root ginger
3 bunches of spring onions, roughly chopped
½ tsp whole white peppercorns

Soup
2 fresh sweetcorn cobs
225g fresh white crab meat
5 tsp cornflour
1 tsp very finely chopped root ginger
2 spring onions, cut into 2.5cm pieces and finely shredded lengthways
1 tbsp light soy sauce
1 tbsp Chinese rice wine or dry sherry
1 egg white, lightly beaten
Salt and black pepper

Put the chicken stock in a pan with the ginger, spring onions and peppercorns. Bring to the boil and cook for 20 minutes for the flavours to infuse, then strain.

Meanwhile, stand the sweetcorn cobs up on a board and slice off the kernels with a large sharp knife. Add the sweetcorn to the stock and simmer for 5 minutes.

Check over the crab meat for any little pieces of shell, keeping the meat in the largest pieces possible.

Mix the cornflour to a smooth paste with a little cold water, stir it into the soup and simmer for 2 minutes. Stir in the crab meat, ginger, spring onions, soy sauce and the rice wine or sherry, then season with salt and some pepper to taste. Simmer for 1 minute.

Now give the soup a good stir, remove the spoon and slowly trickle in the beaten egg white so that it forms long, thin strands in the soup. Simmer for about 30 seconds and then serve at once.

There are some dishes that people love, but I have to admit to being a bit sniffy about. Nachos used to be a case in point. I thought that all that melted cheese over tortilla chips seemed a bit unhealthy – an example of Tex-Mex fast food – but then I discovered that the dish was invented by a maître d' called Ignacio (Nacho) Anaya García in 1943 in the Mexican city of Piedras Negras. When some unexpected guests arrived and the chef was nowhere to be found, Ignacio had to rustle something up quickly, so cut some fried tortillas into triangles, sprinkled them with grated cheese, then baked them and served his creation with pickled jalapeños. Nachos are described as 'loaded' when other things are added; in this instance, some tomato salsa, soured cream and avocado.

LOADED NACHOS WITH CHEDDAR & JALAPEÑOS SERVES 4–6

300g plain or lightly salted
  tortilla chips
250g mature Cheddar or
  a mixture of Cheddar
  and mozzarella, grated
50g pickled jalapeños, sliced
75g soured cream
1 large avocado, diced
Chopped fresh coriander,
  to garnish

Tomato salsa
2 large tomatoes,
  finely chopped
½ small red onion,
  finely chopped
Handful of fresh
  coriander, chopped
1 green chilli, chopped
¼ tsp salt
Juice of a small lime

Preheat the oven to 200°C/Fan 180°C.

Spread half the tortilla chips over an ovenproof serving dish (a lasagne dish is fine). Top with half the grated cheese, half the jalapeños and then the remaining tortilla chips. Scatter over the rest of the cheese and bake for 10–12 minutes until the cheese has melted.

Meanwhile, mix the salsa ingredients in a bowl.

When the cheese has melted, remove the dish from the oven and dollop over teaspoonfuls of soured cream, distributing them evenly. Scatter over the salsa, diced avocado, the rest of the jalapeños and the chopped coriander. Serve at the table with napkins and side plates – this can be messy!

This may not appear on lists as one of the nation's favourite dishes but it's certainly one of the favourites in my restaurants, and it's been on the menu for at least twenty years. In the last year, probably due to global warming, bluefin tuna have been appearing in ever-increasing numbers off the southwest coast of the UK and recently a small quota was allowed. We got our first bluefin in October 2023 and for me, enjoying a slice of perfectly fresh tuna loin was like being back in Tsukiji market in Tokyo. This dish made with it was ethereal.

SEARED TUNA SALAD WITH GUACAMOLE SERVES 4

450g tuna loin fillet
Oil, for brushing
4 coriander sprigs, to garnish
Salt and black pepper

Guacamole
1 jalapeño chilli, deseeded
    and finely chopped
½ small white onion,
    finely chopped
1 large avocado,
    or 2 small ones
Juice of ½–1 lime
Small handful of fresh
    coriander, chopped

Sauce
1 tbsp dark soy sauce
1 spring onion, shredded
¼ jalapeño or green chilli,
    deseeded and chopped
Juice and zest of ½ lime
½ lemongrass stalk, outer
    leaves removed, finely sliced
1 tsp finely chopped root ginger

Heat a ridged cast-iron griddle pan until very hot. Brush the tuna with oil and season liberally with salt and black pepper. Cook the tuna for 1–1½ minutes on each side – the centre of the tuna should remain raw. Remove from the pan and season again, then leave to cool completely. Refrigerate, if preparing in advance.

For the guacamole, pound the chopped chilli with the onion and quarter of a teaspoon of salt with a pestle and mortar. When they have broken down into a lumpy paste, add the avocado flesh and break it up roughly with a fork. Stir in the lime juice to taste, then add the chopped coriander.

In a separate bowl, mix all the sauce ingredients together with 50ml of water.

Slice the tuna into 5mm slices and arrange them, slightly overlapping, on cold plates. Add a spoonful of guacamole to each serving, then drizzle with the sauce. *Recipe photographs overleaf.*

In my cookbook *Seafood Lovers' Guide*, I introduced my recipe for prawn cocktail with what was almost a polemic against the deconstructed versions. Surely, I concluded, the whole point of the dish is that it should be served in some sort of glass used for cocktails. I still feel that is the case if you're using the small sweet prawns from the North Atlantic, but Mitch Turner, the chef at my restaurant Bannisters Port Stevens in New South Wales, whose recipe this is, pointed out that the cocktail glass presentation didn't really do justice to the big tiger prawns that you get in Australia – and here now too. With these, go for the deconstructed, I say. And if you don't believe me, look at the picture.

DECONSTRUCTED PRAWN COCKTAIL SERVES 4

1 baby cos lettuce, thinly sliced
1 Lebanese/baby cucumber, peeled and sliced
20 king prawns, cooked, peeled and deveined, tails left on
Salt
Cayenne pepper
Lemon wedges

Lemon dressing
Squeeze of lemon juice
50ml olive oil
Pinch of sugar

Marie Rose sauce
125g mustard mayonnaise (see p.267 or use Hellman's)
1½ tbsp tomato ketchup
1 tsp Tabasco
¼ tsp smoked paprika (pimentón)
Pinch of cayenne pepper
2 tsp lemon juice
1 tbsp brandy

Mix all the ingredients for the Marie Rose sauce together – you're aiming for a dropping consistency. Season with salt to taste.

Whisk the lemon juice and olive oil together to make the dressing and season with sugar and salt to taste.

Toss the lettuce with the lemon dressing and place in the middle of each plate. Fan the cucumber slices on one side and add 5 king prawns to each serving. Place a large spoonful of Marie Rose sauce over the prawns.

Season with salt and cayenne pepper and serve with lemon wedges.

CHARLECOTE MILL

I feel about Charlecote Mill a bit like I do about Agas. I love Agas but I gave mine up about twenty years ago because I realised there were far easier ways to cook than on something also designed to heat your room and water. And as I learnt, when you incorporate a boiler and pipe into your system, the heat of the Aga is diminished for ever. Yet I still miss its dark-blue presence in our kitchen – the warmth, standing chatting with my bum on the towel rail – and I have to say, nothing tastes as good as a stew that's been slow-cooked in the bottom oven.

Charlecote Mill is near Warwick. It's known as a double-sized, undershot, lowland water mill and it dates back to the early eighteenth century. It was a working mill for many decades but by 1960 it had been left derelict and was not used again for years, except to feature in a television adaptation of *The Mill on the Floss* in 1978. Repairs were made and the mill's fortunes subsequently revived, then in 2012 it was taken over by its current owner, Karl Grevatt.

Within minutes of arriving at Charlecote Mill I had the same sense of comfort as from having an Aga in the house, and I could sense the goodness of the flour that Karl was producing. The old red bricks, the pulleys, the wooden machines and the smell of wheat dust and river water all added up to a feeling that with Karl's flour I was going to bake some of the best bread I'd ever made. The mill also brought back memories of our farm in Oxfordshire where we ground our corn for cattle feed using an old blue Fordson Major tractor with a belt driving a Minnesota Mining and Manufacturing Company corn grinder. Maybe I have an over-enthusiasm for old machinery – I used to take my sons to tractor rallies all over Cornwall – but there was something in that flour mill that made me value its product far and above anything that comes from modern steel rollers.

I asked Karl what he had done before taking on the water mill. A carpenter by trade, he's worked in historic building conservation, on projects ranging from the repairing of the Royal Pew in the Chapel Royal at Hampton Court Palace to rebuilding a listed pigsty. It soon became clear to me that operating this mill meant much more to him than just keeping history alive. Karl clearly relished everything about it and had enjoyed repairing the wide timbers on the floor, the sack hoist and the winnowing machine, all driven by one of the two giant water wheels. Actually, I was thinking that in another life there would be nothing I'd like more than keeping a mill like this running, hearing the water rushing through and driving those massive wheels. I would

'I was thinking that in another life there would be nothing I'd like more than keeping a mill like this running, hearing the water rushing through and driving those massive wheels.'

become like Karl, in love with the personality of the mill. I completely understand why people rebuild things like Spitfires or steam engines. Have you ever watched *The Repair Shop* and seen the love that's poured into restoring those treasures?

For me, the flour from that mill is a story in itself and I have indeed baked some excellent bread from it. Karl's regular customers include 600 local families, two Michelin-star restaurants and a number of artisan bakeries and farm shops. His flour, milled with the stone mills, has a stronger flavour than ordinary flour and because of this the local Indian community say that it's very similar to the flour they used back home for making chapatis. Interestingly, they are now his biggest market and chapati flour has become the core of the business, which reminded me of the way Lake District farmers James and Helen Rebanks (see page 165) found a whole new market for their mutton with the Asian community.

I loved standing with Karl while the whole building hummed and vibrated as the mill wheel turned. It took him some time to learn the whole process, but now he says he recognises the vibrations, the feeling, sound and smell of the mill and all this tells him what to do if something isn't quite right. He also finds himself speaking to the mill quite often and is so in tune with it. As we talked, Karl was constantly listening to the sound of the flour coming into the bag at the bottom and making minute adjustments to its coarseness or fineness. It was wonderful to see someone who so clearly loves the work he does and takes such pride in every detail.

One of the big changes I'm observing in the way we eat out these days is the trend towards small sharing plates. The origin of this comes from Spanish tapas or pinchos. I really like the way these dishes are just served as they are ready and not as part of a conventional first or main course. The ingredients of this recipe are a homage to those Spanish tapas flavours. The dish comes together very quickly and can be stretched to feed more by serving with rice. I've called this a cazuela because I like to serve it in those little traditional earthenware dishes.

CHICKPEA, CHORIZO & RED PEPPER CAZUELA

SERVES 4–6 AS A STARTER OR A FEW MORE WITH DRINKS

3 tbsp extra virgin olive oil
1 red onion, chopped
1 garlic clove, chopped
   or grated
1 tsp hot smoked paprika
   (pimentón)
150g chorizo, diced
1 tbsp dry sherry
2 x 400g tins of chickpeas,
   drained
2 tomatoes, finely chopped
100g roasted red pepper,
   from a jar, diced
Small handful of parsley,
   chopped
Salt and black pepper

To serve
Crusty bread

Heat 2 tablespoons of the oil in a pan, add the red onion and garlic and fry over a medium heat until softened. Add the paprika and chorizo and fry for a minute or so, then add the sherry and allow it to bubble up.

Add the chickpeas, tomatoes and red pepper and fry for a few more minutes to heat everything through. Season with salt and pepper, then stir through the parsley and remaining tablespoon of olive oil. Serve in small shallow bowls with crusty bread to mop up the juices.

The people at the Eusebi Deli in Glasgow (see page 194) told me about a great mozzarella maker in East Acton called La Latteria. You might ask what a mozzarella maker is doing there, but the founder, Simona Di Vietri, explained that success with this cheese is all about the quality of the milk and in the UK it's really good. She sources the milk from small sustainable local farms and was quite dismissive about the need for buffalo milk. Her cheese is gorgeous and this salad reminds me of lovely sunny lunches in Sydney. I've said to grill the peaches and ciabatta on a griddle pan but if you fancy lighting a barbecue, particularly a charcoal one, the result is extra special.

MOZZARELLA SALAD WITH GRILLED PEACHES & HONEY SERVES 2

2 slightly underripe peaches,
    cut into quarters and
    stones removed
1 tsp olive oil
Leaves from a few thyme sprigs
Good handful of salad leaves,
    such as rocket, pea shoots
    or lamb's lettuce
Handful of cherry tomatoes,
    halved
2–4 slices of prosciutto or
    Parma ham, torn into pieces
125–150g ball of mozzarella
1 tbsp clear honey
A few tbsp extra virgin olive oil
1 tsp balsamic vinegar
A few basil leaves, torn
Flaked sea salt and black pepper

Griddled bread
2 large slices of ciabatta
    or a ciabatta roll cut in
    half through the middle
1 large garlic clove, bashed
2 tbsp extra virgin olive oil

Brush the peach pieces with olive oil. Place them on a preheated griddle pan and grill for 5–7 minutes until softened slightly and lightly charred. Transfer the peaches to a plate and season with thyme leaves and some black pepper, then set aside while you prepare the bread.

Toast the bread on the griddle until it is lightly charred and starting to crisp. Rub both cut sides with the bashed garlic clove and brush with extra virgin olive oil.

Put the salad leaves, cherry tomatoes and torn prosciutto in a serving dish. Add slices of peach and the mozzarella torn into large pieces. Drizzle with the honey, olive oil and vinegar, then scatter over basil leaves and flaked sea salt. Serve at once with the griddled bread.

While I was filming tripe and black pudding in Bury Market, I recalled a quote from Anthony Burgess of *A Clockwork Orange* fame who was born nearby. He said: 'I am sometimes mentally and physically ill for Lancashire food — hot-pot, lobscowse and so on — and I have to have these things. I'm loyal to Lancashire, I suppose, but not strongly enough to wish to go back and live there.' And I can understand how he felt, because things like black pudding, tripe and eccles cakes are just so special to that part of the country. Thank goodness these days people are far less dismissive of such foods, even black pudding. I've never written a recipe for scotch eggs before, but I've always enjoyed eating them in pubs and I decided to add black pudding to the mix. Do feel free to leave it out if you prefer and use extra sausage meat, but it does give the scotch egg extra flavour and a moister texture. For me, piccalilli is a must with the eggs. You probably have your favourite but there is a recipe for mine in the back of the book.

SCOTCH EGGS WITH FENNEL, SAUSAGE MEAT & BLACK PUDDING MAKES 6

6 medium eggs,
    at room temperature
1 tbsp vegetable oil
1 shallot, finely chopped
400g sausage meat
Small handful of parsley,
    chopped
1½ tsp fennel seeds, crushed
200g black pudding, crumbled
100g plain flour
100g panko or dried
    white breadcrumbs
2 medium eggs, beaten
1 litre sunflower or
    vegetable oil, for frying
Salt and black pepper

To serve
Piccalilli (see p.269),
    mustard or chutney
Pickled onions

Bring a pan of water to the boil, add a teaspoon of salt and lower in the eggs. Boil for 6–6½ minutes, then immediately cool them under cold running water until they are completely cold. Peel the eggs and set them aside.

Heat the oil in a small pan and gently fry the shallot until translucent, then leave to cool. Put the sausage meat in a bowl and add the fried shallot, chopped parsley and crushed fennel seeds, then season with salt and pepper and mix well. Fold in the crumbled black pudding.

Put the flour, breadcrumbs and beaten eggs on separate plates. Lightly flour the peeled eggs. Divide the sausage mixture into 6 balls. Flatten one in your hand, then add an egg and shape the sausage mix around the egg. Repeat with the remaining eggs. Roll each egg in flour, then beaten egg and finally in breadcrumbs.

Heat the oil to 160°C in a large, deep pan. Using a slotted spoon, lower in the eggs, 2 at a time, and cook for 8–10 minutes until they are deep golden brown and crisp. Drain on kitchen paper and serve with piccalilli, chutney or mustard and pickled onions or as part of a ploughman's lunch with bread and cheese.

Yoven Virasami is head chef at our restaurant in Marlborough. He's originally from Mauritius and was extremely happy to know that I'd been there and enjoyed the local cuisine. Situated as it is right out in the Indian Ocean, Mauritius is bound to be influenced by the cooking of the Indian subcontinent and these excellent crunchy fritters are a typical example. What's great about Yoven is that he loves his own country's cuisine but he's also very happy to cook my dishes and does them extremely well. That's something I really respect in good chefs – that they have tremendous creative ability but are also happy to cook what I want in the way I want it.

YOVEN'S DHAL FRITTERS

SERVES 4–6 AS A STARTER OR LIGHT LUNCH

250g yellow split peas
½ onion, finely chopped
½ tbsp chilli flakes
30g spring onions,
    finely chopped
15g fresh coriander,
    finely chopped
1½ tsp salt
10 fresh or frozen curry leaves
750ml vegetable or sunflower
    oil, for frying

Virasami chutney
6 ripe medium tomatoes,
    roughly chopped
2 green chillies, chopped
1 tsp chopped fresh coriander
1 medium onion, finely sliced,
½ tsp vegetable oil
Salt

Soak the split peas in a large bowl of water for at least 8 hours or overnight. By the next morning, the peas should have puffed up slightly and the water will have reduced. Drain the peas, tip them into a food processor and blitz to form a coarse paste that clumps together. Tip this into a large bowl and add all the remaining fritter ingredients, except the oil, and mix well. Leave to rest for an hour, then mix again.

Take a tablespoon of the mixture in your hand and press it firmly into a ball weighing about 25g. Continue to make about 20 balls.

Make the chutney by putting all the ingredients into a blender and pulse until you have a paste.

Pour some vegetable oil into a deep pan, wok or deep-fat fryer and heat to 180°C. Fry the fritters in batches of 5 or 6 for 3–5 minutes until golden-brown. Drain on kitchen paper and serve immediately with the chutney.

I've mentioned how much Sas and I enjoyed a sharing board and dinner rolls at the Devonshire in Soho recently and what a good option I think this is as a first course. I've come up with a recipe for some soft rolls to accompany the board, inspired by those we ate that night and really, apart from whisking some feta cheese with Greek yoghurt and olive oil, there's nothing much else to do, except arrange the elements in a charming and colourful way. It's good if you can bake the rolls just before everyone arrives. You can also use this recipe to make six burger buns.

SHARING BOARD WITH OLIVE OIL & ROSEMARY DINNER ROLLS

SERVES 6 (2 ROLLS EACH)

Olive oil & rosemary rolls
500g strong white bread flour,
    plus extra for dusting
7g sachet fast-action dried yeast
1½ tsp salt
2 tsp caster sugar
300ml lukewarm water
4 tbsp olive oil, plus 2 tbsp
    for brushing the tops
2 tbsp chopped rosemary,
    plus extra for sprinkling on top
Sea salt flakes

Sharing board options
80g prosciutto
80g salami
½ cured chorizo ring, sliced
3–4 slices of cooked ham
150g Dolcelatte
100g Parmesan, broken
    into chunks or sliced
150g olives
100g whole almonds
6 figs, halved
250g cherry tomatoes
30g fresh basil, torn into sprigs
100g sweety drop peppers
120g mini gherkins
150g artichoke hearts
Small bunches of grapes
Olive oil and balsamic vinegar dip

Whipped feta
100g feta cheese
6 tbsp Greek yoghurt
2 tbsp olive oil
Chopped parsley
Pine nuts or chopped pistachios

For the rolls, mix together the flour, yeast, salt and sugar in a large bowl. Add the water, 4 tablespoons of oil and 2 tablespoons of rosemary and use your hands to bring everything together into a rough dough. Transfer to a board and knead for about 10 minutes until soft and elastic. You can do this in a food mixer with a dough hook if preferred. Wash and lightly oil the bowl, put the dough back in it and cover with a clean tea towel. Leave to rise for about an hour or until doubled in bulk.

When the dough has risen, knock it back and lightly knead for a minute or so before dividing it into 12 pieces. Line a tin (about 20 x 30cm in size) with baking parchment. Roll each piece of dough into a ball and arrange them in the tin, then cover again with the tea towel. Leave to rise for a further 45–60 minutes or until doubled in size.

Ten minutes before baking, preheat the oven to 195°C/Fan 175°C. Brush the tops with another tablespoon of oil and sprinkle with rosemary and sea salt. Bake for about 20 minutes until well risen and lightly coloured. Keeping the 12 rolls on the parchment and joined together, transfer to a wire rack, then drizzle with a little more oil. Leave to cool for about 15 minutes.

For the whipped feta, whizz the feta, yoghurt and olive oil in a food processor until soft and smooth. Add an extra tablespoon of olive oil if needed to loosen it. Drizzle with olive oil and top with parsley and some pine nuts or chopped pistachios.

Arrange the charcuterie, cheese and other items on your board as beautifully as you can and serve with the whipped feta and the warm rolls to tear and share. *Recipe photographs overleaf.*

Arancini should be the size of tennis balls, as I discovered on a visit to Palermo for the series I did called *Long Weekends*. I observed at the time that they made much more sense like this, making a sustaining lunch a bit like a Cornish pasty. I had to include 'nduja somewhere in this book, as its popularity has made it a bit of a modern food phenomenon. With its exquisite flavour of Calabrian red chillies and cured meat made from pork cheeks, it makes a perfect filling for these risotto balls.

ARANCINI WITH 'NDUJA, MOZZARELLA & BASIL MAKES 6

Risotto
About 1.2 litres chicken stock
40g butter
300g Arborio or Carnaroli
   risotto rice
1 tsp fennel seeds, crushed
50g Parmesan or Pecorino
   cheese, freshly grated
1 egg yolk
Salt and black pepper

To coat and deep-fry
1 large egg
75g panko breadcrumbs
1–1.5 litres vegetable oil

Filling
75g mozzarella,
   cut into 6 chunks
60g 'nduja
A few basil sprigs

Heat the stock for the risotto in a saucepan. Melt the butter in a wide pan over a medium-low heat, add the rice and stir well. Add a ladle of hot chicken stock along with the fennel seeds and stir until absorbed, then continue to add the stock a ladleful at a time, stirring until it is all absorbed; this should take about 20 minutes. Add the grated cheese and the egg yolk, season with salt and pepper and stir. Spread the rice out on a lightly greased baking tray, leave to cool, then transfer it to the fridge and chill for 2 hours or overnight.

When you're ready to coat and fry, beat the egg in one bowl and put the breadcrumbs in another. With damp hands, scoop a sixth of the risotto on to your palm. Using the back of a spoon, spread and press the rice over your palm and closed fingers. Then add a chunk of the mozzarella, a spoonful of 'nduja and a basil leaf in the middle and mould the rice around them to form an arancino about the size of a tennis ball. Set aside. Repeat until all 6 are made. Preheat the oven to 130°C/Fan 110°C.

Heat the oil in a deep pan to 160°C – check with a probe or a sugar thermometer. Have a plate lined with kitchen paper at the ready. Roll each ball in beaten egg, then in breadcrumbs and lower 2 at a time into the oil using a slotted spoon. Cook for 8–10 minutes until golden brown all over, then transfer to the lined plate to absorb excess oil. Keep the arancini warm in the oven while you fry the rest. Serve warm or cool.

FISH & SHELLFISH

You may notice that there are more than a couple of recipes for breadcrumbed fish in this book. One of my purposes in life is to persuade us Brits to eat more fish and I finally realised that everybody loves fish coated in breadcrumbs, particularly if those breadcrumbs are the Japanese, very dry-roasted panko sort which give such an amazingly crisp finish. Hence, you'll find recipes for fish finger sandwiches, smoked haddock fishcakes and scampi in the basket, all with that lovely coating. Of course, the ideal accompaniment to breadcrumbed and fried fish is tartare sauce and I'm very proud of the one we serve in our fish and chip shops. It's made with olives, capers, gherkins, parsley and proper mayonnaise, but I seem to have upset quite a few people when I put the price of a portion up from 75p to £1. The complaint was that many other fish and chip shops give it away. My point was that I'm not a fan of the vinegary white slush that is often sold as tartare sauce. Need I say more? Also in this chapter are some classics with fish such as Dover sole and John Dory, as well as new favourites such as a seafood ramen and a dish of teriyaki salmon baked in foil.

I'm forever enthusing about the flavour to be found in the heads and shells of langoustines and other prawns, and this shellfish stock is the star feature of my arroz roja. This Spanish seafood rice dish is very similar to a paella, except that the beautifully flavoured red rice and the seafood are cooked separately. The Spanish call this style *arroz a banda*, which means 'rice on the side' and I think gives you the best of both worlds. I'm very fond of this recipe and for me, it has to be served with aioli – or allioli as the Spanish call it.

ARROZ ROJA SERVES 4

8 frozen langoustines
6 tbsp olive oil
1 onion, finely chopped
4 garlic cloves, finely chopped
1 tsp smoked paprika
    (pimentón)
1 tbsp tomato paste
250g ripe tomatoes, chopped
1 roasted red pepper, from
    a jar or freshly roasted,
    chopped into 1cm pieces
Pinch of chilli flakes
400g short-grain paella rice,
    such as Calasparra
300g haddock fillet, skin
    on, cut into 4 pieces
Salt and black pepper

Shellfish stock
1 tbsp olive oil
1 small onion, chopped
1 carrot, chopped
1 celery stick, chopped
Langoustine heads and shells
60ml white wine
1.5 litres fish stock or water
1 fresh tarragon sprig
150g tomatoes,
    roughly chopped

To serve
Aioli (see p.267)
Handful of parsley,
    roughly chopped
1 lemon, cut into wedges
    (optional)

Start by peeling the langoustines. Set aside the flesh and roughly chop the heads and shells for the stock.

For the shellfish stock, heat the tablespoon of olive oil in a large pan. Gently fry the onion, carrot and celery for a few minutes until softened. Add the chopped langoustine heads and shells and fry for a couple of minutes. Add the white wine, bring to the boil and cook for a minute, then add the fish stock or water, tarragon and chopped tomatoes. Cook for 40 minutes, then push everything through a fine sieve over a large pan, pressing with a wooden spoon to extract as much flavour as you can. You need 1 litre of finished stock for 400g of rice, so top it up with a splash of water if under a litre.

In a large (28–30cm) frying pan or a shallow flameproof casserole dish, heat 4 tablespoons of the olive oil over a medium heat. Add the onion and fry gently for about 5 minutes, then add the garlic and fry for a minute without browning. Stir in the pimentón, tomato paste, chopped tomatoes, chopped red pepper, chilli flakes, shellfish stock and rice, then season with salt and pepper.

Stir once, then bring up to a boil and simmer vigorously for about 6 minutes. Turn the heat down and cook for a further 12 minutes, until the stock is absorbed and the rice is pitted with small holes.

A few minutes before the rice is due to finish cooking, heat the remaining olive oil in a separate pan over a medium-high heat. Add the haddock, skin-side down, and cook until the flesh is opaque. Add the langoustines and cook for about 30 seconds or so, until pink, turning them once. Divide the rice between 4 bowls and top each with a piece of haddock and 2 langoustines. Garnish with aioli and chopped parsley and a wedge of lemon if you like.

Baking fillets in foil is one of the simplest and most satisfying ways of cooking fish, as it's quick and all the succulence is retained. What's more, there's no aroma of fried fish in the house if that's something that bothers you. I do think that oily fish like salmon go particularly well with Japanese flavours of soy, ginger and the slightly oxidised, nutty flavour of sake or Chinese Shaoxing wine. I've suggested dry sherry as an alternative if you can't find sake or Shaoxing wine.

TERIYAKI SALMON PARCELS WITH PAK CHOI & BROWN RICE

SERVES 2

2 x 125–150g salmon fillets
1 tsp vegetable oil
1 garlic clove, chopped
2 heads of pak choi, cut into
   quarters through the root,
   or 250g chard
1 tsp soy sauce
¼ tsp chilli flakes
1 spring onion, finely sliced
½ tsp toasted sesame seeds

Teriyaki marinade
1 tbsp brown soft sugar
2½ tbsp soy sauce
1–2cm root ginger, grated
1 tsp toasted sesame oil
1 tbsp sake, Shaoxing wine
   or dry sherry
1 star anise, broken

To serve
Brown rice (see p.264)

First make the teriyaki marinade by simply mixing everything together. Set aside.

Preheat the oven to 200°C/Fan 180°C. Line a baking tray with a large sheet of foil and put the salmon fillets on top. Spoon over the teriyaki marinade, then pull in the sides of the foil to create a parcel and scrunch the top to seal. Place in the hot oven for 10–12 minutes.

Heat the oil in a pan, add the garlic and fry gently until fragrant but not browned. Add the pak choi or chard, soy sauce, chilli flakes and 1 or 2 tablespoons of water. Put a lid on the pan and cook over a medium heat until the leaves have wilted and the stems are tender.

Divide the greens between 2 plates, top with a piece of salmon and spoon over the juices, discarding the star anise. Scatter over the slices of spring onion and the sesame seeds and serve with rice.

In my last book *Simple Suppers* I wrote about the open heart surgery I'd had at the Royal Brompton Hospital in London. I'd been particularly impressed the evening before the operation by being served some simply fried haddock with soy sauce, olive oil and red peppers, but then my hopes of great hospital food had been dashed by some overcooked lamb and very gluey mint sauce. Rather than be affronted by my criticism of hospital food, the Brompton asked me to supply a couple of recipes and this fish and pasta dish is one of them. It's designed to be economical and very easy to make, and with the pesto sauce it's really quite delicious.

COD WITH LINGUINE, TOMATO & COARSE GREEN PESTO SERVES 2

300g dried linguine
300g skinless cod fillet,
    cut into 2cm chunks
1–2 tbsp olive oil
75g cherry tomatoes,
    quartered
Salt and black pepper

Pesto
15g fresh basil
1 garlic clove, chopped
80ml olive oil
25g Parmesan, freshly grated
25g blanched almonds

Put all the pesto ingredients in a food processor and blend for about 15–20 seconds; the mixture should be fairly coarse.

Bring a large pan of well-salted water (1 teaspoon of salt per 600ml) to the boil and cook the pasta for 7–9 minutes until al dente. Drain and tip the pasta back into the pan, then stir through the pesto.

While the pasta is cooking, heat the olive oil in a non-stick frying pan over a low-medium heat. Add the pieces of cod and cook very gently for 3 minutes, then add the quartered cherry tomatoes. Add the cod and tomatoes to the pasta, season with salt and pepper, then mix gently to combine. Serve immediately.

I originally wrote this recipe thirty or so years ago when there was still plenty of sea trout in the Camel estuary in Cornwall. Sadly, numbers have diminished to the extent that I probably only get a decent-sized sea trout, or peel as they're called locally, a couple of times a season. The same proved to be the case when I went coracle fishing on the Tywi river in Carmarthen. Fortunately, we did net a couple of salmon which we had to put back, but the catch completed the excitement of night-time fishing on a sweet-smelling river with high banks on either side. You can buy farmed sea trout, but if you find it hard to get or inordinately expensive, salmon works well. We've taken to serving this dish at The Seafood Restaurant under a cloche of fresh smoke. This is a bit of a MasterChef trope and some find it a little on the naff side. I argue that it's now so old-fashioned it's rather sweet.

CHARGRILLED, LIGHTLY SMOKED SEA TROUT WITH CHIVE DRESSING SERVES 4

50g salt
400g sea trout or salmon
   fillet, skinned and cut
   into 4 equal pieces
Woodchips
Olive oil

Chive dressing
1 small bunch of chives
1 small shallot, finely chopped
90ml extra virgin olive oil
1 tbsp white wine vinegar
½ tsp salt

Tomato salad
6 tomatoes, finely sliced
1 small red onion,
   finely sliced
Pinch of caster sugar
1 tbsp extra virgin olive oil
1 tsp sherry vinegar or
   balsamic vinegar
Handful of parsley or
   basil, chopped or torn

To serve
Potato salad (see p.262)

To make a light brining liquid, dissolve the salt in 600ml of water in a shallow dish. Add the fish, cover and leave for 20 minutes. Drain and pat the fish dry.

For the chive dressing, set aside 4 of the chives for a garnish and finely slice the rest. Mix them with the shallot, olive oil, vinegar and salt.

For the salad, arrange the sliced tomatoes on a serving plate and scatter over the sliced red onion. Season well with salt, pepper and sugar, then dress with oil and vinegar and garnish with the herbs.

Preheat a barbecue. Throw a handful of woodchips on to the coals and close the lid.

Brush the pieces of smoked trout with a little oil. Place the pieces diagonally on the barbecue grill and cook for a couple of minutes on each side until lightly marked by the ridges and the centre of the fish is just warm.

Spoon some of the chive dressing on to each plate and put the pieces of trout on top. Garnish with the remaining chives and serve with the tomato salad and a potato salad.

This is one of the dishes I enjoyed when I visited the Houria Café in Bristol (see pages 144–45) while filming my *Food Stories* series. I just added an egg to the fishcakes, which I believe Kim said you could do if you felt it necessary. I do find that salt cod or *bacalao* is not to everyone's taste, but I think that this recipe with chilli, lime and garlic is such a different kind of fishcake to what we're used to that it's well worth making. Shop-bought salt cod needs to be soaked for twenty-four hours, but I would suggest preparing your own. Simply cover a cod, haddock or hake fillet with salt, leave it overnight and then wash off the salt with copious amounts of water. No soaking needed.

KIM'S SALT COD FISHCAKES WITH CHILLI & CORIANDER

MAKES 8–10

300g salt cod, soaked for 24 hours if shop-bought (change water every 8 hours)
600g floury potatoes, such as Maris Pipers, peeled and cut into chunks
1–2 red chillies, chopped
1 garlic clove, chopped
1 red onion, finely chopped
Large handful of fresh coriander, chopped, plus extra to garnish
1 egg, beaten
Zest of 1 lime
50g plain flour, plus extra for dusting
1 litre vegetable oil, for deep-frying
Salt and black pepper

To serve
Lemon wedges
Aioli (see p.267)

Bring a pan of water to simmering point, add the soaked fish and poach for 10 minutes.

Boil the potatoes in salted water until tender, then drain well and leave them to dry in a colander for a few minutes.

Mash the potatoes, then add the cooked, flaked salt cod, chopped chillies, garlic, red onion, coriander, beaten egg, lime zest and flour. Season with salt and pepper and mix well.

Form the mixture into oval patties and dust them with flour. Fill a large, deep pan two-thirds full with oil and heat to 160°C. Add 3 or 4 fishcakes and deep-fry for 3–4 minutes or until golden-brown. Drain on kitchen paper and keep them warm while you cook the rest. Serve with lemon wedges, aioli and sprigs of coriander.

I have a bit of a love/hate relationship with craft ale. I'm of a generation that prefers delicate English hops to the enormous power of American ones. When we were filming at the Wild Card Brewery in Walthamstow recently, brewer Jaega Wise gave me bags of both English and American hops to sniff and the American hops were like New Zealand Sauvignon Blanc in the strength of their aroma. But when it comes to using beer in a sauce for fish that extra fragrance makes all the difference. I'm very fond of this simple treatment for a great fish like John Dory, which is perfectly complemented by the bitterness of the beer and the smokiness of the bacon.

PAN-FRIED JOHN DORY WITH BEER, BACON & LETTUCE SERVES 4

4 x 175g fillets of John Dory
   or gurnard, skin on
50g butter, melted
750g cos lettuce, shredded
75g rindless smoked streaky
   bacon, chopped
1 onion, finely chopped
1 garlic clove, finely chopped
   or grated
300ml good chicken stock
300ml pale ale
2 tbsp sunflower oil
Small handful of parsley,
   chopped
Salt and black pepper

Place the fish fillets on a plate and sprinkle them generously with salt. Leave them for about 15–20 minutes, then rinse off the salt and pat the fish dry with kitchen paper. Brush the fish with a little of the butter and season with pepper, then set aside.

Heat some of the butter in a frying pan, add the bacon and fry until golden and crisp. Add the remaining butter and gently fry the onion and garlic for 5 minutes until softened. Add the chicken stock and beer to the pan and cook over a high heat until the liquid has reduced by three-quarters. Turn the heat down as much as possible, cover the pan and leave the sauce over the low heat while you cook the fish.

In a separate pan heat the oil over a medium heat and cook the fish, skin-side down, for about 6–7 minutes until the skin is crisp and the fish is opaque.

Stir the lettuce into the sauce and allow it to wilt, then stir in the chopped parsley and season, if needed, with salt and pepper. Divide the lettuce and bacon between 4 plates, top with a piece of fish and spoon the sauce around. Serve immediately.

THE TWO RAYS

I have to be honest and say that Morecambe is not the thriving seaside resort it once was. There are a lot of empty stores – and plenty of nail bars, tattoo parlours and charity shops – but no one can take away the beauty of the view of the bay, with its miles and miles of sand flats stretching into the horizon, and the distant pleasure of the hills and mountains of the Lake District. I was there twenty years ago with Chalky, my Jack Russell, and I went out fishing on Ray Edmondson's home-made boat. Now I was back to film one of my favourite delicacies for which Morecambe is justly famous – brown shrimps.

Ray has sold his boat and these days concentrates on running his fish shop and potting the shrimps landed for him by another Ray – Ray Porter. It was very reassuring to be back in the familiar conviviality of Ray's shop with its smells of smoked fish and the spices for his very special potted shrimps. Traditionally, the shrimps are boiled in sea water before being preserved in spiced clarified butter.

Ray's potted shrimps are still exquisite. He wouldn't, of course, give me his recipe, but he didn't deny that mace and white pepper were a big part of it, and he did let me have a sniff of his tub of spice mixture. I asked him there and then if he would supply my restaurant in Padstow, which he now does, and his shrimps are flying out. They are a real delicacy, and it was sad to hear from Ray how few people fish for them these days.

I did, though, meet Ray Porter, the other Ray, who is still fishing for brown shrimps. It's a bit of a depressing sign of the times but for insurance reasons I wasn't allowed to accompany Ray for the five-mile journey out across the sand, pebbles and mudflats of Morecambe Bay to dredge for shrimps. He doesn't use a boat and instead has his own very inventive solution. I have to admit that when I first saw his tractor, which seemed to be held together by rust, and his wonderfully Heath Robinson home-made shrimp dredger, made mostly of old nets and scaffold poles, which I remember describing as a work of art, I felt slightly relieved I wasn't going out with him.

Ray drives out over the flats on his tractor and finds the channels that are left filled with water at low tide where a lot of shrimps become trapped. He dredges these with his net trolley pulled by the tractor, all the time keeping a close eye on the incoming tide. I asked Ray if he had ever broken down out there. He said, 'Oh yeah, once or twice'. I was pleased to see that a second equally rusty and ancient tractor driven by his chum was going out with him, but it's salutary to remember that twenty-one Chinese cockle gatherers lost their lives some years ago in those treacherous waters due to the fast-moving tides. Locals say that the Morecambe tide can come in 'as fast as a horse can gallop'.

Meeting with both the Rays was a moving experience. OK, so our country is not in the best shape at the moment, but I sort of feel that the tougher times are for people, the more interesting and heroic they appear. For me, both Ray Edmondson in his fish shop, surrounded by an area with a lot of urban decay, and Ray Porter with his rusty old tractor and dredger show such ingenuity and determination; their humorous optimism certainly lifted my spirits.

When you go supermarket shopping these days you see chiller cabinets full of fishcakes, testimony to how much they are loved. It was noticeable when I made three television series in Cornwall recently that one of the most popular of the dishes I cooked was a recipe from the late Barry Humphries for fishcakes with capers and pink peppercorns. My wife, Sas, and I have such fond memories of Barry and so here is another fishcake that I'm sure he would have liked, containing smoked haddock which goes very well with leek and strong Cheddar cheese. The only thing I like to serve with these is some soft lettuce.

SMOKED HADDOCK, LEEK & CHEDDAR FISHCAKES

MAKES 6 (SERVES 3–6 DEPENDING ON APPETITE)

600g King Edward potatoes, peeled and cut into 5cm chunks
350g undyed smoked haddock
10g butter
225g leeks, trimmed and finely sliced
75g vintage or mature Cheddar, coarsely grated
Small handful of parsley, chopped
Salt and black pepper

To coat and fry
50g plain flour
2 eggs, beaten
100g panko breadcrumbs
Vegetable oil, for frying

Cook the potatoes in a pan of well-salted water (1 teaspoon of salt per 600ml) for 10–15 minutes. Once tender, drain the potatoes and leave them to dry in a colander for a few minutes, then mash well.

While the potatoes are cooking, put the haddock in a pan with about 500ml of water. Bring to the boil, then immediately turn off the heat, cover the pan with a lid and leave to stand for 8–10 minutes. Lift the fish out and when it's cool enough to handle, flake the flesh and discard the skin and any bones.

In a separate pan, melt the butter and gently fry the leeks until soft, allowing any liquid to evaporate.

In a large bowl, mix the potatoes with the cooked leeks, grated cheese and parsley, then season generously with salt and black pepper. Gently mix in the fish, trying not to break the flakes up too much. Form into 6 patties.

Put the flour, beaten eggs and breadcrumbs in 3 separate bowls. Dip each patty into the flour, egg, then breadcrumbs. Heat the oil in a large frying pan and fry the fishcakes for 4–5 minutes on each side, until golden. Keep the fishcakes warm in a low oven if frying in a couple of batches.

We serve scampi in the basket with chips and tartare sauce at our pub, The Cornish Arms in St. Merryn. Sadly, it always seems to revert on the menu to scampi in *A* basket, although I've repeatedly tried to get it changed. For me, this is a classic dish of the seventies when breaded scampi (langoustine tails) were served in a reed basket with chips and a sachet of sauce. It was convenient pub grub you could serve in the bar. I believe the original dish came from Italy and was made with scampi from the Venice lagoon and served with thin chips. Over the years it's been made more and more economical so that the scampi is of the smallest type, and indeed there was a suggestion that monkfish was sometimes used as a substitute but that's now almost as expensive. I decided to make scampi using really good-quality langoustines from a fishing trip out on Holy Loch near Glasgow and I'm including a recipe for my own tartare sauce. It was utterly spectacular. Do reserve the langoustine shells for shellfish stock, which can be frozen and used in risottos, sauces or soups.

SCAMPI IN THE BASKET WITH TARTARE SAUCE SERVES 2

10 fresh (or frozen and
    defrosted) langoustines
    or 12 king prawns, defrosted
50g plain flour
1 egg, beaten
75g panko breadcrumbs
1 litre sunflower oil,
    for deep-frying
Salt

Tartare sauce
300ml mustard mayonnaise
    (shop-bought or see p.267)
2 tsp finely chopped
    green olives
2 tsp finely chopped gherkins
2 tsp finely chopped capers
2 tsp finely chopped parsley
2 tsp finely chopped chives

To serve
Lemon wedges
Chips (shop-bought
    or see p.115)

Mix all the ingredients for the tartare sauce together and refrigerate until needed.

Peel the langoustines or king prawns and devein if you like.

Put the flour, beaten egg and breadcrumbs in separate bowls. Take the langoustines or prawns and dip them first in the flour, then beaten egg, then breadcrumbs and set aside.

Fill a large, deep pan two-thirds full with oil and heat to 180°C. Carefully lower in the langoustine or prawns 3 or 4 at a time and fry for 1–2 minutes until golden and crisp. Drain on kitchen paper, sprinkle with salt and keep them warm while you cook the rest.

Serve with tartare sauce, lemon wedges and some chips if you like.
Recipe photographs overleaf.

I thought that potato cakes, or tattie scones as they're known in Scotland, would be great served with excellent smoked salmon from the Isle of Bute and they certainly are. They do need to be made with freshly cooked mashed potato, as the mixture is more malleable. When I cooked this dish, I used standard red beetroot, but I particularly like the pretty candy beetroot that Jan Smith, the food stylist who makes my food look so wonderful, used for this photo.

TATTIE SCONES WITH SMOKED SALMON & BEETROOT, RADISH & FENNEL SALAD SERVES 4

Tattie scones
500g floury potatoes,
    such as Maris Pipers
    or King Edwards, peeled
25g butter
2 spring onions, finely sliced
100–150g self-raising flour
Salt and black pepper

Beetroot salad
1 small raw beetroot, peeled
4 radishes, trimmed
1 small fennel bulb
2 tbsp cider vinegar
1 tbsp olive oil
1 heaped tsp brown soft sugar
1 tsp chopped dill

To serve
4 tbsp crème fraiche
2 heaped tsp creamed
    horseradish
150–200g smoked salmon
    or trout
Extra dill or fennel fronds
Lemon wedges

Cut the potatoes into chunks, put them in a pan of well-salted water (1 teaspoon of salt per 600ml) and cook until tender. Drain and leave to dry for a minute or so. Mash until lump free, then stir in the butter and when it has melted, stir in the spring onions and enough flour to make a non-sticky dough. Season with salt and pepper, then leave until it's cool enough to handle.

Put half of the mixture on a floured board and roll it into a disc about 20–25cm in diameter – cut around a plate to help you make a neat round. Cut this into quarters and, using a fish slice, transfer these to a dry frying pan over a medium heat – the idea is to toast the scones rather than fry them. Cook for 3–4 minutes on each side until golden, then remove and keep warm. Repeat with the remaining mixture.

While the scones are cooking, finely slice each vegetable for the salad separately, preferably on a mandoline. Put them in a bowl, mix gently and dress with the cider vinegar, oil, sugar and chopped dill.

In a separate bowl combine the crème fraiche and horseradish, then season with salt and pepper.

Serve 2 tattie scones on each plate, top with the salad and a dollop of the crème fraiche mixture. Add slices of smoked salmon or trout, a few fronds of dill or fennel and some lemon wedges.

FISHING AND THE FREEDOM OF THE SEA

I suppose I'm a real sucker for regional accents in the UK. And as accents go, I find the Suffolk one very pleasant to the ear – a mix of a bit of London with a lot of rural thrown in. It's the accent of people you can trust and Dean Fryer, fisherman of Aldeburgh, is just that sort of person. I first met him when filming twenty years ago with Chalky, my intrepid Jack Russell terrier, who would jump on a boat as casually as if leaping over a stream.

I returned to Aldeburgh when filming my *Food Stories* series. It was great to see Dean again after all that time. He was a lot more grizzled but still lean and droll and absolutely as happy to be fishing now as he was then. He still says he wouldn't want to do anything else. Over those twenty years, I wonder how many nets he's hauled, boxes he's lifted, fish he's skinned and gutted? How tired he will have got and yet there's nothing he would prefer to do in life. I had to ask why something so tough is so good to do? Dean, like so many other fishermen, says it's the freedom of being away from land. But I do wonder if in some sort of curious way there is a metaphysical, mystical quality about the sea that gets under your skin, almost like an addiction. I know that so many people who've been brought up the sea crave its presence in their lives. It's almost a sine qua non of living by the sea – you have to go back to it.

There's a fantastic poem by Robert Frost that I quoted in my very first television series. The first verse strikes me as very true.

> The people along the sand
> All turn and look one way
> They turn their back on the land
> They look at the sea all day
>
> Robert Frost, 'Neither Out Far Nor In Deep', 1936

The reality for Dean is that he is catching what is really quite a good quantity of fish; not outrageous amounts but enough to sell to his customers on the shore each day. He supplies local restaurants in Aldeburgh and beyond. How lucky are the people here to have a fisherman like Dean.

'I do wonder if in some sort of curious way there is a metaphysical, mystical quality about the sea that gets under your skin, almost like an addiction.'

This isn't a book about being pessimistic, but Dean did mention that he was the last one catching and selling fish on the beach in Aldeburgh. It may be more the unwillingness of people to take up such a life rather than a shortage of fish. But, like many a fisherman, Dean did mention all the red tape that's involved now in the job and this must put many a young man or woman off taking up the trade.

Not so for Mary Galloway from Holy Loch in Argyll who we also filmed with. At fifty she gave up teaching because she had promised herself she would have a new career when she reached that age. But who would have thought she would choose fishing? She obviously loves it and when we met, explains that it's all about 'the pure enjoyment of being out on the water'. She added: 'It's so peaceful. If you leave the house in the morning with a problem, after half an hour out here you don't have a problem.'

She and fellow fisherman Alastair catch langoustines, most of which they sell in Spain, and they make a good living from it. I know how good their langoustines are because I received a package of the live shellfish from the Loch and turned them into scampi in the basket, a dish I recall with great nostalgia from the seventies. It may be a little on the pricey side but with some good home-made tartare sauce, what could be nicer. I'd like to encourage more of us in this country to cook with langoustines.

My son Jack introduced me to the delight of using miso in sauces with fish dishes. I guess if you wanted a prime example of umami flavour it would be miso. He's also shown me how using western flavours like cream and chicken stock in conjunction with what is a paste made from fermented soybeans is a great example of how fusion can really work.

HAKE WITH WHITE MISO, SHIITAKE & SOBA NOODLES SERVES 2

150g soba noodles
2 tbsp olive oil, for frying
2 x 125g hake fillets, skinned
60g shiitake mushrooms, sliced
1 rounded tbsp white
    miso paste
100ml chicken stock
60ml double cream
85g (2 good handfuls) fresh
    spinach leaves
Juice of ½ lemon
2 spring onions,
    finely shredded
Black pepper

Cook the noodles according to the instructions on the packet, then drain and set aside.

Heat oil in a large non-stick frying pan. Add the fish fillets to the pan, with the sliced shiitake around them, and gently fry over a low-medium heat for 2–3 minutes on each side. Transfer the fish and mushrooms to a warm plate and cover with foil to keep warm while you finish the noodles.

Add the miso, stock and cream to the frying pan along with the noodles and spinach leaves and toss everything together. Allow the spinach to wilt and the liquid to reduce until it just coats the noodles, then add some of the lemon juice and season with pepper.

Divide the noodles between 2 shallow bowls and top each serving with a piece of hake and some shiitake. Add more lemon juice, garnish with shredded spring onions, then serve.

This recipe comes from my friend Mark Hix's restaurant, The Oyster & Fish House in Lyme Regis. Pollock is a popular catch in Lyme Bay and it's becoming more and more common on menus because, like cod, it produces nice thick flaky fillets. I remember as a child catching small pollock when we went mackerel fishing and bringing them back to our house on Trevose Head. My mother wasn't very keen on pollock and used them for fishcakes, but I've since learned that larger pollock can be as tasty as cod, and so it was when Mark cooked this dish for me when we filmed in his kitchen for *Food Stories*. Fresh cockles can be a bit hard to find, but mussels are a good substitute.

PAN-FRIED POLLOCK WITH SEASHORE VEGETABLES & COCKLES SERVES 4

4 x 150–175g pollock fillets from a large fish, pin-boned
1–2 tbsp vegetable oil
250g live cockles
50ml white wine or cider
100g samphire or other sea vegetables, such as sea aster, sea purslane, etc.
120g unsalted butter, diced
Salt and black pepper

Lightly season the pollock with salt and pepper. Heat a little oil in a large non-stick pan and fry the pollock fillets for about 3 minutes on each side, until they are nicely coloured and just cooked through. If the fillets are very thick you will need to finish them in a hot oven for a further 5–10 minutes to ensure they're cooked.

Meanwhile, rinse the cockles thoroughly in cold running water to get rid of any sand, then put them into a large pan with the white wine. Cover with a tight-fitting lid and cook over a high heat until they begin to open, shaking the pan and giving them an occasional stir.

Drain the cockles in a colander, reserving the liquid. Pour the cooking liquor back into the pan, add the samphire or other sea vegetable and butter and keep stirring until the butter has melted. Tip the cockles back into the pan (they will not need seasoning as the samphire will do that) and stir well.

To serve, carefully transfer the pollock to serving plates and spoon over the cockles, samphire and sauce. *Recipe photographs overleaf.*

In a book with a subplot about the nation's favourite dishes, it would be remiss not to include ramen, which is extraordinary because perhaps even only five years ago very few people would know what this was. Now, thanks to Wagamama and other Japanese-style restaurants, ramen noodles are immensely popular. Beef and chicken ramen are what people generally go for, but I think the same basic stock with prawns, scallops and salmon dropped in at the last minute is a fabulous alternative. I was originally intending to write this to include a handful of mussels, because I often make ramen with some I've picked on the beach after a swim, but I realise that often you can only buy mussels in quite large net bags, so that doesn't seem practical.

SALMON, PRAWN & SCALLOP RAMEN SERVES 2

500ml chicken stock
1 tbsp soy sauce
5g piece of kombu (dried kelp)
20g root ginger, sliced
    (no need to peel)
1 large garlic clove, sliced
200g ramen noodles (wheat,
    brown rice or buckwheat)
50g mangetout
6 large cooked, peeled prawns
    (defrosted if frozen)
50g bean sprouts
2 large scallops, sliced
    horizontally into 3 thin 'coins'
100g salmon fillet, thinly sliced
1 egg, soft-boiled and cooled
1 spring onion, sliced thinly
    on the diagonal
Coriander leaves, to garnish
1 red chilli, finely sliced,
    or chilli oil

Pour the stock into a pan, add the soy sauce, kombu, sliced ginger and garlic, then bring it to the boil. Turn the heat down and simmer for 15–20 minutes to allow the flavours to infuse. Once the stock has infused, remove the kombu, ginger and garlic with a slotted spoon and discard. Keep the stock over a low heat.

Cook the noodles according to the packet instructions, then drain and refresh under cold water.

A few minutes before the noodles are ready, turn up the heat under the stock. Add the mangetout and cook for 2 minutes, then add the prawns and cook for another minute. By this time the mangetout should be tender and the prawns hot.

Divide the noodles between 2 bowls and top with bean sprouts, scallops and thinly sliced salmon. Ladle over the hot stock (which will quickly cook the scallops and salmon) and divide the mangetout and prawns between the bowls. Cut the egg in half and add a half to each bowl, then garnish with the sliced spring onion, coriander leaves and chilli slices or oil. Serve immediately.

I'm very pleased to have discovered that these sandwiches are one of the nation's favourite dishes and they're even better made with home-made fish fingers, rather than shop-bought. Good white bread is the best thing here.

FISH FINGER SANDWICHES SERVES 4

500g thick pollock or
    haddock fillet, skinned
2 tbsp plain flour
1 large egg, beaten
About 70g panko breadcrumbs
3–4 tbsp vegetable or
    sunflower oil
Lemon juice
Salt and black pepper

To serve
8 slices of white bread, buttered
Lettuce leaves
Tartare sauce (see p.65)
    or ketchup

Cut the fish into 2cm strips and season them with salt and pepper. Dust the strips with flour, then dip them in beaten egg and roll in panko breadcrumbs. Set aside.

Heat the oil in a frying pan and cook the fish fingers for 2 or 3 minutes on each side until crisp and golden. Sprinkle with a little salt and lemon juice, then assemble the sandwiches with lettuce and tartare sauce or ketchup. *Recipe photographs overleaf.*

The older I get the keener I am to keep ingredients out of recipes instead of adding them. This is as simple a recipe for fish pie as you can imagine, but if the fish is good (and that includes the smoked fish which must be of the best quality), there is no better fish dish in the world than British fish pie —with boiled eggs and parsley, of course. I know some people don't like boiled eggs in their pie, so by all means leave them out. Also referring back to my last book *Simple Suppers*, you can make this recipe easier by topping the pie with bought puff pastry instead of mash. You can use haddock or hake instead of cod, but I just think the smoked haddock is essential.

CLASSIC FISH PIE SERVES 4

1 small onion, thickly sliced
2 cloves
1 bay leaf
600ml whole milk
300ml double cream
450g unskinned cod fillet
225g undyed smoked
   haddock fillet
4 eggs
100g butter
45g plain flour
Handful of curly parsley,
   chopped
Freshly grated nutmeg
1.25kg floury potatoes,
   such as Maris Piper or
   King Edward, peeled
   and cut into chunks
1 egg yolk
Salt and freshly ground
   white pepper

Stud a couple of onion slices with the cloves. Put the onion slices in a large pan with the bay leaf, 450ml of the milk, the cream, cod and smoked haddock. Bring just to the boil, then simmer for 8 minutes.

Lift the fish out on to a plate, strain the cooking liquor into a jug and set it aside. When the fish is cool enough to handle, break it into large flakes, discarding the skin and bones. Sprinkle it over the base of a shallow 1.75 litre ovenproof dish.

Boil the eggs for just 8 minutes, then drain and leave to cool. Peel the eggs and cut them into chunky slices, then arrange on top of the fish.

Melt 50g of the butter in a pan, add the flour and cook for a minute. Take the pan off the heat and gradually stir in the reserved fish cooking liquor. Put the pan back on the heat and slowly bring to the boil, stirring all the time. Leave the sauce to simmer gently for 10 minutes to cook the flour. Remove from the heat, stir in the parsley and season with a grating of nutmeg, salt and white pepper. Pour the sauce over the fish and leave to cool, then place in the fridge to chill for an hour.

Boil the potatoes for 15–20 minutes. Drain them, then mash and add the rest of the butter and the egg yolk. Season with salt and white pepper, then beat in enough of the remaining milk to form a soft, spreadable mash.

Preheat the oven to 200°C/Fan 180°C. Spoon the potato over the filling and mark the surface with a fork. Bake for 35–40 minutes, until piping hot and golden brown.

Before writing this I asked everyone sitting round the table how they felt about quinoa and Jinny Johnson, who corrects everything I write, said, 'I like it, but I don't lust after it'. But it is good for you – nutritious, rich in fibre and minerals and gluten free, so ideal for anyone who can't tolerate other wheat. But above all I do like the texture. It's quite firm, with the same sort of slight resistance as pearl barley and therefore a perfect foil for this highly colourful salad. Originally a South American grain, quinoa is now also grown in this country.

QUINOA SALAD WITH HOT SMOKED SALMON, LEMON & TARRAGON SERVES 4–6

100g uncooked quinoa
300ml hot water
2 eggs
125g frozen peas
1 tbsp chopped tarragon
Small handful of parsley, chopped
2 little gem lettuces, shredded
150g hot-smoked salmon or roasted salmon
2 spring onions, finely sliced
Salt and black pepper

Dressing
3 tbsp mayonnaise
3 tbsp plain yoghurt
2 tsp fresh lemon juice
3 tarragon sprigs, leaves stripped from stalks and chopped

Put the quinoa in a pan and add the hot water. Cover the pan and simmer for 12–15 minutes until all the water is absorbed but the grains still have some bite. Season with salt and pepper, fluff up the quinoa with a fork and leave to cool completely.

Boil the eggs for just 8 minutes, then drain and leave to cool. Peel the eggs and cut them into quarters.

Put the peas in a bowl, pour boiling water over them, then drain. Combine the cooled quinoa with the peas, tarragon and parsley.

Mix together the dressing ingredients, adding a splash of water to thin it down a little if necessary. Season to taste.

Scatter the shredded lettuce over a serving platter or shallow bowl. Add the quinoa, peas and herbs, then flake the salmon over the top and add the quartered hard-boiled eggs. Sprinkle over the spring onions and drizzle with some of the dressing. Serve immediately with any remaining dressing on the side.

'Meunière' means miller's wife in French, so this is fish cooked in the style of the miller's wife – dusted with flour. This is still my favourite fish dish and Alex Smith, the designer of my books, adores it too. I always say if you think you don't like fish, order yourself a Dover sole if you can afford it. I would defy anybody not to love this dish. As with many a prime cut of meat or poultry, the simplest ways of cooking fish are generally the best.

DOVER SOLE À LA MEUNIÈRE SERVES 2

2 x 400–450g Dover soles,
    trimmed (see method)
    and skinned
25g plain flour
4 tbsp olive oil
50g unsalted butter
2 tsp lemon juice
1 tbsp chopped parsley
2 tsp capers
Salt and freshly ground
    white pepper

To serve
Lemon wedges
Sautéed potatoes (see p.261)

To trim a sole, take a pair of sharp scissors and cut the frilly fins and the fleshy bones off both sides. You want to cut about 4cm off all round so that you are left with just the 4 fillets on the backbone. Repeat with the other sole. Season the fish with salt and white pepper. Dip both sides of each fish into flour, then pat off the excess.

Heat the oil in a large well-seasoned or non-stick frying pan. Add one of the soles, lower the heat slightly and add a small piece of the butter. Fry the fish over a moderate heat for 4–5 minutes, without moving it, until richly golden.

Carefully turn the fish over and cook for a further 4–5 minutes until golden brown and cooked through. Transfer it to a serving plate and keep warm. Repeat with the second fish.

Discard the frying oil. Add the remaining butter to the pan and allow it to melt over a moderate heat. When the butter starts to smell nutty and turn light brown, add the lemon juice, parsley, capers and some seasoning. Pour some of this beurre noisette over each fish and serve with lemon wedges. Good with some sautéed potatoes.

I've always felt that cooking fish and chips at home is not really doable, simply because of the large amount of oil you need for deep-frying a few decent portions of fish. Cod bites, on the other hand, are much easier to cook and as long as you use fairly good-sized chunks you still get that lovely silky flakiness from the fish.

COD BITES WITH BEER BATTER SERVES 4

600g skinless cod fillet
100g plain flour
1 litre vegetable oil,
    for deep-frying
Salt and black pepper

Batter
200g plain flour
¼ tsp salt
½ tsp baking powder
275ml cold beer

For the batter, sift the flour into a large bowl with the salt and baking powder. Use a balloon whisk to incorporate the beer until you have a smooth batter, then set aside.

Fill a large, deep pan two-thirds full with oil and heat to 190°C.

Cut the cod into chunks roughly 5cm square. Season the chunks with salt and pepper and dip them into the flour, then shake off any excess and dip them into the batter. Fry them in batches for 2–2½ minutes, until crisp and deep golden in colour. Drain on a plate lined with kitchen paper and lightly sprinkle with salt.

Serve immediately with tartare sauce (see page 65) and some chips (see page 115) and mushy peas (see page 259), if you like.

VEGETARIAN DISHES

I wonder if there's a more popular vegetarian dish in this country than falafel. If you love them as much as I do, you have to experience the falafel of a lifetime at Mr Falafel's café in Shepherd's Bush market. He piles his golden, deep-fried falafel into wraps with layers of hummus, tomatoes, parsley, pickles and tahini sauce. It's a gorgeous mix of crispness, crunchiness, spiciness and vegetable cleanness, but if you're clumsy like me, beware of dribbling the hummus all over Mr Falafel's floor. Falafel are a perfect example of food that just happens to be vegan and there are a few other vegan recipes in this chapter. It's been explained to me, by the way, that the term plant-based is not synonymous with vegan. It simply means that the majority of what you eat is food derived from plant sources and that suits me these days. For instance, both the biryani made with aubergines and the paneer jalfrezi in this chapter were dishes that I originally wrote with meat in them and now I prefer the veggie versions. May I also draw your attention to the matar kulcha, which I sampled on a trip to Old Delhi recently, and hugely enjoyed.

This is based on a recipe I wrote for my book *Rick Stein's India,* but I've adapted it to make it vegetarian. After some experimentation, I came to the conclusion that aubergine was far and away the best vegetable to use here. I know I'm saying this, but it is really good.

AUBERGINE BIRYANI SERVES 6–8

750g aubergines,
    cut into 3–4cm dice
10 whole cloves
6cm cinnamon stick
5 green cardamom pods,
    bruised with a rolling pin
2 medium tomatoes, chopped
200g baby spinach leaves,
    washed
600g basmati rice
Salt

Marinade
250ml natural yoghurt
6 garlic cloves, finely crushed
30g root ginger, finely grated
3 green chillies, finely chopped,
    with seeds
1 tsp Kashmiri chilli powder
1 tsp ground coriander
½ tsp ground turmeric

Fried onions
150ml vegetable oil
3 medium onions, thinly sliced
1 tsp garam masala
1 tsp cumin seeds

To assemble
100g ghee
Pinch of saffron soaked
    in 4 tbsp warm milk
    for 15 minutes
2 tsp rose water (optional)
20g cashew nuts and 20g
    pistachios, dry-roasted
    in a hot pan until golden

To serve
Cucumber and mint raita
    (see p.267)

Combine the marinade ingredients in a bowl, add the diced aubergines and toss to coat. Set aside to marinate for 30 minutes.

For the onions, heat the oil in a sturdy pan over a medium heat until hot but not smoking. Add the onions and fry for 10–15 minutes or until deep golden-brown, then add the garam masala and cumin seeds. Remove the onions with a slotted spoon, drain on kitchen paper, then set aside. Pour off all but about 3 tablespoons of the oil from the pan into a jug to use another time.

Add the cloves, cinnamon and cardamom to the pan and fry for 1 minute. Add the aubergine and marinade, then bring to a simmer and stir in the tomatoes and a teaspoon of salt. Simmer over a medium heat for 15 minutes until the aubergine is tender and the sauce is clinging to it. Stir in the spinach – add a splash of water to the pan if the spinach catches on the bottom – and cook for a few more minutes until wilted. The sauce should be almost dry and just coating the aubergine. Keep it warm over a low heat while you cook the rice.

Bring a large pan of water to the boil and add salt – 1 teaspoon per litre of water. Add the rice and cook for 5–7 minutes until just tender but still firm, then drain well.

Assemble the biryani straight away. Pour about 3 tablespoons of water and half the ghee into a deep, heavy-based pan. Spoon in a third of the rice, then a third of the onions and half the aubergine. Sprinkle in some saffron milk, a little rose water, if using, and a few cashew nuts and pistachios. Then spoon in another third of rice, more onions, the rest of the aubergine, more saffron milk and rose water and a few more nuts. Finally, add the rest of the rice, saffron milk and rose water and most of the remaining onions.

Drizzle the remaining ghee around the edges of the rice so it drips down the inside of the pan. Cover with a well-fitting lid and place over a high heat to get the ghee hot and some steam going – lift up the lid to check. As soon as you see steam rising, turn the heat down very low and cook for 30 minutes. Spoon out on to a large serving platter and scatter with the rest of the fried onions and toasted cashews and pistachios. Serve with raita.

You could almost call this dish mushy peas Indian style. The peas are flavoured with garam masala and a 'temper' of sizzling-hot fried chillies and chopped ginger. They are topped with a hot potato cake called a pethis and with chopped tomato, onion and coriander, plus optional jini sev, which looks like fried vermicelli. I was shown how to make it by the chef at Bundobust in Leeds. At this restaurant, Gujarati vegetarian dishes are paired with craft beer in a fascinatingly informal setting that's far removed from the red or purple flocked wallpaper style beloved of first-generation Indian restaurants in this country.

RAGHDA PETHIS SERVES 4–6

Raghda
300g marrowfat peas
2 tsp bicarbonate of soda
2 tsp salt
1 tbsp garam masala

Temper
2 tbsp sunflower oil
3–4 green chillies, chopped
30g root ginger, chopped
½ tsp ground turmeric

Pethis
500g potatoes,
    such as Desirée
    or Rooster, peeled
½ tsp salt
1 tsp garam masala
¼ tsp ground turmeric
2 green chillies, chopped
1 tbsp chopped fresh
    coriander
3–4 tbsp sunflower oil,
    for frying

To serve
½ red onion, chopped
1 large tomato, chopped
Sweet tamarind sauce
Jini sev (optional)
Small handful of fresh
    coriander, chopped

For the raghda, put the marrowfat peas in a bowl, cover with cold water and add the bicarbonate of soda. Leave to soak overnight or for at least 8 hours.

Once soaked, drain the peas well and rinse thoroughly. Transfer the soaked peas to a large pan with the salt and garam masala and add 700ml of water. Bring to the boil, then lower the heat to medium-low and cook the peas for 20–30 minutes until very soft and mushy. Mash some of the peas with a potato masher or with the back of a spoon, then leave to simmer over a low heat while you make the tempering.

For the temper, heat the oil in a pan over a medium heat. Once the oil is hot, add the chopped chillies and ginger, fry for 1 minute, then add the turmeric. Cook for 30 seconds, then transfer the tempering to the simmering ragdha in the pan.

For the pethis, cut the potatoes into chunks, put them in a pan of cold water and bring to the boil. Cook for 5 minutes, then drain. Leave the potatoes to cool, then grate them into a bowl and add the salt, spices, chillies and coriander. Mix everything well to form a smooth dough.

Make 6 equal-sized patties from the potato mixture – they should be 70–75g each in weight. Heat the oil in a non-stick pan over a medium-high heat, then add the prepared patties. Cook for 4–5 minutes on each side until golden brown.

Serve the raghda in bowls and place a pethis on top of each serving. Garnish with chopped onion, tomato, sweet tamarind sauce, jini sev, if using, and fresh coriander.

I'm sure you'll love the photographs of this dish. It was so enjoyable assembling all those different colours of root vegetables and by roasting the veg first, the flavours are deepened and sweetened. The carrot top pesto is remarkably delicious too, and I find it very satisfying to use the tops rather than chuck them away.

CARROT, BEETROOT & RED ONION TARTE TATIN SERVES 8–10

40g butter, at room
   temperature, plus
   extra for greasing
10–12 rainbow carrots,
   scrubbed, trimmed
   and halved lengthways
3 medium beetroots,
   scrubbed or peeled
   and sliced into rounds
   3–4mm thick
4 tbsp olive oil
2 star anise, bashed
2 tsp brown soft sugar
3 large red onions, sliced
1 garlic clove, chopped
400–500g puff pastry
Flour, for dusting
Salt and black pepper

Carrot top pesto
Good handful of green
   carrot tops, washed
   and roughly chopped
1 garlic clove,
   roughly chopped
30g vegetarian Parmesan-
   style cheese, grated
7–8 tbsp olive oil
15g pine nuts

You will need a 26–27cm round pie tin or ovenproof frying pan, or a rectangular roasting tin measuring about 18 x 25cm. Grease it generously with butter. Preheat the oven to 200°C/Fan 180°C.

Put the carrots and the beetroot slices in a large roasting tin and add the 4 tablespoons of olive oil, the star anise and a teaspoon of the sugar. Season with salt and pepper, then, using your hands or wooden spoons, toss the whole lot together until the vegetables are coated in the oil and seasonings. Roast for 15–20 minutes.

Meanwhile, melt the 40g of butter in a pan and add the sliced red onions and garlic with the remaining teaspoon of brown sugar. Cook over a low-medium heat until the onions are very soft and sweet, then remove from the heat.

Place the carrots over the base of the buttered tin or pan in an attractive pattern, then add the beetroot slices on top and the red onions. Season with salt and pepper as you go.

Lightly dust your work surface, with flour, then roll out the puff pastry until it's a little larger than your pan to allow for shrinkage. Place the pastry over the vegetables, tucking it down the sides of the pan, then trim off any excess. Bake the tart for 25–30 minutes until the pastry is crisp and risen.

Remove the tart from the oven and allow it to cool a little before turning out. Meanwhile, put all the pesto ingredients in a blender and blitz. Add a splash of water if necessary to get a drizzling consistency.

Carefully cover the tin or pan with a large serving plate or board and invert to turn the tart out. You may need to rearrange a few of the vegetables with a palette knife to tidy it up.

Serve slices of the tart with the pesto drizzled over or alongside and a green salad. *Recipe photographs overleaf.*

I wrote this recipe for a Greek-style filo pie after going to Mary Quicke's farm and dairy near Exeter. It was a thoroughly enjoyable visit and I was very impressed with Mary's resistance to automation, favouring the manual skills of her very experienced team. Very laudable when you consider the enormous popularity of her Cheddar cheese. I took some home to make this vegetarian pie, but when I cooked it for an episode of *Food Stories*, I came a little unstuck as it was pointed out by more than one viewer that the cheese I used is made with rennet. I am pleased to suggest using one of her lovely vegetarian cheeses called Double Devonshire instead for this pie.

CHEESE, POTATO & SPINACH FILO PIE SERVES 6

600g potatoes, peeled
260g spinach, washed
25g butter
1 large onion, sliced
175ml double cream
2 medium eggs, beaten
½–1 tsp English or
    Dijon mustard
7–8 sheets of filo pastry
50g butter, melted
175g mature or vintage
    vegetarian Cheddar or
    Quicke's Double Devonshire,
    coarsely grated
Salt and black pepper

Cook the potatoes in a pan of well-salted water (1 teaspoon of salt per 600ml), then drain and leave to cool. Cut them into slices 5–6mm thick. Wilt the spinach in a pan, then squeeze out as much of the liquid as possible.

Heat the butter in a pan, add the onion and fry until soft and golden. Mix the cream with the eggs and mustard and season with black pepper.

Preheat the oven to 210°C/Fan 190°C. Take a 23–25cm pie dish and layer 4 sheets of filo in the base, brushing each sheet with melted butter and alternating directions. Allow the excess to overhang the sides. Add half the sliced potato, scatter over some onion and spinach, then add half the cream mixture and cheese. Season with salt and pepper. Repeat with the remaining potato, spinach and onion, season again with salt and black pepper and top with remaining cream and cheese.

Fold over the overhanging filo and then top with a further 3 or 4 sheets of filo, again brushing each one with melted butter. Brush the top of the pie with butter.

Bake for 10 minutes in the preheated oven, then cover the top with a sheet of foil to prevent it burning. Turn the oven down to 190°C/Fan 170°C and cook for a further 20–25 minutes. Leave to cool in the tin for 5–10 minutes before serving.

Mr Falafel's café at Shepherd's Bush market makes the best falafel I've ever tasted and this is my version of his recipe. May I add here that the noun 'falafel' can be countable or uncountable. In general, the plural is also falafel, but in more specific contexts, it can also be falafels; for example, in reference to various types of falafels or a collection of falafels.

FALAFEL WITH TAHINI DRESSING MAKES 12

200g dried chickpeas
½ tsp bicarbonate of soda
30g flatleaf parsley
15g dill
1 small onion, roughly chopped
1 green chilli, roughly chopped
3 garlic cloves, peeled
1 tsp salt
2 tsp ground cumin
Large pinch of cayenne
    or Aleppo pepper
1 tsp baking powder
Sunflower or olive oil, to cook

Tahini dressing
3 tbsp tahini
Juice of 1 lemon
1 tsp ground cumin
1 large garlic clove, grated
75ml very cold water
Salt and black pepper

Serving options
4–6 pitta breads or flatbreads
Hummus
½ red onion, thinly sliced
Cabbage or salad leaves,
    finely shredded
Chopped flatleaf parsley
Pickled turnip (see p.268)
Cucumber, thinly sliced
Whole pickled chillies
Pinch of cayenne or
    Aleppo pepper

The day before you want to make the falafel, put the dried chickpeas in a bowl and cover with plenty of cold water. Stir in the bicarbonate of soda and leave to soak.

The next day, drain the chickpeas and rinse them, then tip them into a food processor. Add the parsley, dill, onion, chilli, garlic, salt, cumin and cayenne or Aleppo pepper and pulse until you have a mixture with a texture similar to breadcrumbs or couscous. Chill for an hour.

Put all the dressing ingredients in a blender and whizz until smooth.

Add the baking powder to the falafel mixture and stir thoroughly. Shape the mixture with your hands into walnut-sized balls and flatten them slightly.

You can cook the falafel in several different ways. To deep-fry, pour sunflower oil into a large pan to a depth of 7–8cm. Heat to 170°C, then add the falafel in batches and fry for 2 minutes on each side. When they are crisp and golden, transfer them to a plate lined with kitchen paper.

To shallow fry, heat 4–5 tablespoons of sunflower oil in a non-stick pan and fry the falafel for 3–4 minutes on each side until they are crisp and golden.

To bake, preheat the oven to 200°C/Fan 180°C. Brush the falafel with olive oil, place them on an oiled tray and bake for 10 minutes. Turn them over or shake the tray and cook for a further 10 minutes until golden – they won't be as dark as the deep-fried version.

Lightly toast and split the pitta breads or flatbreads. Add as many of the serving options as you like, plus 2 or 3 falafel, then drizzle over some of the tahini dressing. Season with a pinch of cayenne or Aleppo pepper and serve immediately.

I wrote this recipe for my book *Rick Stein's India* about ten years ago and it has proved to be very popular. It's basically an Indian take on a stir-fry and at the time I was a little nervous about it because, although based on some dishes I'd eaten, it is very much my own version. I suppose in this context it's my homage to some of the great vegetarian curries that I've had recently while filming in Leicester. This recipe is specifically for paneer, the Indian cheese, which is easy to get now and available in most larger supermarkets. I have on occasion, though, used the Cypriot cheese halloumi, which is similar, though saltier.

PANEER JALFREZI SERVES 2–4

3 tbsp vegetable oil
1½ tsp cumin seeds
1 dried Kashmiri chilli,
    whole with seeds
25g root ginger, finely shredded
3 small onions, thinly sliced
1 garlic clove, sliced
1 fresh green chilli, chopped,
    with or without seeds
1 red or yellow pepper,
    deseeded and cut lengthways
    into thin strips
1 green pepper, deseeded
    and cut lengthways into
    thin strips
1 tsp salt
½ tsp ground turmeric
1½ tsp Kashmiri chilli powder
250g paneer, cut into
    small cubes
3 tomatoes, cut into strips
1 tsp white or red wine vinegar
½ tsp toasted ground
    cumin seeds
¾ tsp garam masala
    (see p.271 or shop-bought)
Handful of fresh
    coriander leaves

Heat the oil in a heavy-based saucepan over a medium heat. Add the cumin seeds, whole dried Kashmiri chilli and about two-thirds of the shredded ginger, then fry for 30 seconds until aromatic.

Add the onions, garlic and green chilli and fry for 5–6 minutes until the onions are just softening but not browned and still have a little crunch. Add the peppers, salt, turmeric and chilli powder, then fry for a further 3–4 minutes.

Lower the heat, add the paneer to the pan and gently stir everything together for about 5 minutes, then add the tomatoes and a splash of water and heat through. Stir in the vinegar, ground cumin seeds and garam masala, then scatter with the remaining shredded ginger and the fresh coriander before serving.

LEICESTER'S INDIAN FOOD SCENE

Having been to Uppingham School, near Leicester, I've always had a certain fondness for the city, in spite of the fact that it has always been industrial and not particularly, dare I say it, pretty. So it was with some mixed feelings that I came back to Leicester for filming. And I was no more enthused on arrival when I was asked to meet my contact, food writer Gurdeep Loyal, in the middle of an industrial estate – where there was no sign of any food.

Gurdeep, who was born and brought up in Leicester, led me to a kiosk opposite a massive food-processing factory, with trucks going in and out transporting potatoes to the Ginsters pasty company in Cornwall. The kiosk was gaudily painted with pictures of what turned out to be Gujarati vegetarian dishes. It appeared to be shut but there was a little bell to ring for you to order. The shutters would briefly slide open and you gave your order, in my case for mixed puri. The shutters closed again and only opened when the puris – and the very hot *vada pav* Gurdeep ordered – were ready. As always, as soon as I tasted the great food, everything changed for me, and Leicester became the most intriguing city and the little kiosk full of character.

It's almost impossible to overstate the importance of Indian cuisine in our own culture. No wonder that twelve years ago, I decided to film a series in India that had the strapline 'In search of the perfect curry'. David Pritchard, the director of that series, knew before we started that there was no such thing as a curry in India, but it was a perfect way to describe to our compatriots why we were going. I still love the theme song, with an Indian voice saying at the end: 'That's a mind-blasting curry, Ricky'.

It's no surprise that several curries are among the nation's favourite dishes, notably chicken tikka masala, chicken korma and biryani. But of late, as with Italian food and Chinese, Indian food is becoming more and more popular in its regional varieties. When I first filmed in the sub-continent in Bangladesh, the main reason for going there was that Bangladeshis were responsible for a high percentage of all the Indian restaurants in UK. I recently filmed at the two Michelin-starred restaurant Opheem and met chef and owner there, Aktar Islam. Aktar is of Bangladeshi parentage and said that those restaurants of the seventies and eighties, including the Balti restaurants, are now declining in favour of Indian regional cuisine.

Returning to the subject of Leicester, Gurdeep has just written a book called *Mother Tongue: Flavours of a Second Generation* which celebrates his adventurous 'British-Indian' style of cooking. He proved

> 'As always, as soon as I tasted the great food, everything changed for me, and Leicester became the most intriguing city and the little kiosk full of character.'

to be the most knowledgeable guide to the Leicester Indian food scene. From the kiosk, we moved on to a restaurant right in the centre of the city called Chai Paani where I ate masala dosas – big floppy but crisp rice pancakes wrapped round soft potato curry and dipped into various chutneys. I remember thinking at the time that Indian vegetarian cooking doesn't get any better – and this is Leicester! We should be immensely proud of the Indian food produced in this country. I once sat in a Keralan restaurant in south London and watched a group of about a dozen Frenchmen who had clearly flown in just for the food.

By the time we got to our final destination, Bobby's Restaurant – a family-run place that features a special afternoon tea menu – I had certainly had enough to eat and was looking forward to just a couple of sweets such as kulfi and shrikhand and maybe a nice, sweet cup of chai. But owner Dharmesh Lakhani had other ideas. As far as I can remember, I ended up with an Indian version of tea at the Ritz, with three tiers of savoury and sweet items, including paneer pakodas, chocolate barfi and mango shrikhand. I couldn't eat it all, but I loved Bobby's. It felt like a real occasion and the interior looked like a scene from the *Barbie* movie.

I left Leicester feeling that it is one of those cities where people are getting on with their lives and producing things. There's a pleasing optimism about the place.

I only really like butternut squash if it's roasted first, which concentrates the flavour and makes it deliciously sweet, and this technique is successful in a risotto. What I do is mash the roasted squash, but not too thoroughly, so some soft lumps remain in the finished risotto. This can be a good vegan dish if you leave out the cheese and use plant-based butter.

BUTTERNUT SQUASH & SAGE RISOTTO SERVES 4

4 tbsp olive oil
8–10 sage leaves
900–1kg butternut squash, peeled, deseeded and cut into rough chunks
1.5 litres vegetable stock
60g butter
1 banana shallot, chopped
1 garlic clove, chopped
300g Arborio or Carnaroli rice
100ml dry white wine
60g vegetarian Parmesan-style cheese, grated
Salt and black pepper

Preheat the oven to 220°C/Fan 200°C. Heat the oil in a frying pan until hot but not smoking and add 4 whole sage leaves. Fry them until crisp, then set them aside on kitchen paper, ready to garnish the risotto later. Set the pan aside.

Pour the oil from the pan into a roasting tin and add the butternut squash. Slice the remaining sage leaves into thin strips and add them to the squash, then season with salt and pepper. Roast the squash for 25 minutes until golden and tender.

Pour the stock into a pan and bring to the boil. Melt 40g of the butter in the frying pan, add the shallot and garlic and cook gently until softened but not coloured. Add the rice and stir well to coat, then cook until translucent. Add the wine and allow it to bubble up and be absorbed. Start adding the hot stock, a ladleful at a time, waiting until each addition is absorbed before adding the next. Keep stirring for 18–20 minutes until the rice is creamy and the consistency is soupy.

Using a potato masher, mash the roasted butternut squash very roughly and add it to the rice, then fold in the remaining butter and two-thirds of the grated cheese. Season well with salt and black pepper. Serve the risotto in warmed bowls and top each with a little more cheese and a fried sage leaf.

I wrote this recipe after a trip to a tofu factory just outside Leeds – I was so interested to find that perfectly good tofu is now made in this country. The flavour was great but what I also liked was that though much of the process was automated, they cut the tofu by hand, giving it a home-made look and feel. The rest of the recipe is based on a pad Thai I filmed years ago in Bangkok at a stall by the Ghost Gate, so named because it is next to a large cemetery. An excellent location for feeding famished mourners. I like the flavour of the dried shrimp, but feel free to leave it out if you prefer.

PAD THAI WITH TOFU SERVES 2

175g Thai folded rice noodles
4 tbsp vegetable oil, plus 1 tsp
2 tbsp Thai fish sauce
2 tbsp tamarind water (see tip)
½ tsp chilli flakes
2 tbsp sweet chilli sauce
1 tbsp palm sugar or brown
    soft sugar
200g firm tofu,
    cut into 1.5cm dice
1 garlic clove, grated
2 eggs, beaten
50g bean sprouts
1 tbsp dried shrimp (optional)
4 spring onions,
    trimmed, halved and
    shredded lengthways
Small handful of fresh
    coriander, roughly chopped
50g roasted peanuts,
    coarsely chopped

To serve
Lime wedges and extra
    coriander leaves and
    chilli flakes

Bring a pan of water to the boil, drop in the noodles and cook for about 3 minutes until just tender. Drain them well, refresh with cold water, then drain again and toss in a teaspoon of oil to prevent them clumping together. Set aside.

Combine the fish sauce, tamarind water, chilli flakes, chilli sauce and sugar in a small bowl, then set aside.

Heat the 2 tablespoons of the oil in a wok and fry the cubes of tofu in batches until golden. Remove the tofu and set it aside to keep warm.

Add the remaining oil to the wok, add the garlic and stir-fry for 10 seconds, then add the drained noodles and stir-fry for a minute. Push the noodles to one side, add the eggs and scramble them in the base of the wok.

Add the bowl of sauce and combine it with the noodles, then add the bean sprouts, dried shrimp, if using, the fried tofu, spring onions, coriander and peanuts. Mix well and let everything warm through. Divide between warmed bowls and garnish with lime wedges, coriander leaves and chilli flakes.

TIP
To make tamarind water, take 60g of tamarind pulp and put it in a bowl with 150ml of hand-hot water. Work the paste with your fingers until it has broken down and the seeds have been released. Strain the slightly syrupy mixture through a fine sieve into another bowl and discard the fibrous material left behind. The water is now ready to use and can be kept in the fridge for 24 hours.

A great way to use up any bits and pieces of cheese from your cheeseboard or fridge. If including Stilton or other strong blue cheese, you may want to use a smaller percentage compared with Cheddar, Gruyère and so on. Not only is blue cheese strong in flavour, but it can also give the sauce a slightly greyish appearance.

CHEESEBOARD MAC & CHEESE SERVES 6–8

100g butter, plus extra
    for greasing
100g plain flour
1 heaped tsp Dijon mustard
1.3 litres milk
100ml double cream
1 bay leaf
400g of whatever vegetarian
    cheese you have, hard
    or soft
Handful of parsley,
    chopped (optional)
500g dried macaroni
50g panko breadcrumbs
25g vegetarian Parmesan-style
    cheese, grated
Salt and black pepper

Melt the butter in a large pan, stir in the flour and cook for a minute. Add the mustard, then take the pan off the heat and gradually whisk in the milk and cream. Add the bay leaf and put the pan back over a medium heat and stir until the sauce comes to a boil and is thick and bubbling.

Grate any hard cheese and thinly slice or crumble any soft cheese. Add the cheese to the sauce, season with plenty of black pepper and taste. You probably won't need salt as the cheese will be salty enough. If the mixture is lumpy, whizz it with a stick blender to achieve a smooth sauce. Stir in the parsley, if using, and set the sauce aside.

Bring a large pan of well-salted water (1 teaspoon of salt per 600ml) to the boil. Cook the macaroni for 8–10 minutes until al dente, then drain well. Preheat the oven to 200°C/Fan 180°C. Butter an oven dish, measuring about 35 x 20cm.

Combine the macaroni with the cheese sauce and tip the mixture into the greased dish. Mix the panko crumbs and grated Parmesan-style cheese and sprinkle over the top, then grind over some more black pepper. Bake for 25–30 minutes until golden and bubbling and serve with a large green salad.

If preparing this ahead of time and chilling, allow 40–45 minutes to cook from cold.

Memories here of a sunny trip to Southwold in Suffolk and a laudable café called The Canteen, run by Nicola Hordern. The café serves great food, using only the freshest seasonal ingredients from local producers. It was really pretty and when I say that on their website they write: 'spacious outdoor seating – enjoy our bee-friendly garden', I think you can picture how lovely it was. A very simple filling for this tart but absolutely delicious.

RAINBOW CHARD, RED ONION & CHEESE QUICHE SERVES 8–10

Pastry
350g wholemeal plain flour
Piinch of salt
190g cold butter, cubed
35g Pecorino or any vegetarian hard cheese of your choice, grated
4–5 thyme sprigs, leaves removed and chopped
125ml very cold water

Filling
30g butter
500g rainbow chard, stalks chopped and set aside, then leaves chopped
1 red onion, chopped
5 whole eggs
4 yolks
600ml double cream
A small handful of any herbs you like, thyme, chives, etc., finely chopped
150g cheese (Pecorino or any vegetarian hard cheese of your choice), grated
200g curd cheese or crumbled vegetarian feta
Salt and black pepper

To serve
Green salad

For the pastry, put the flour in a bowl with a pinch of salt, add the butter and rub it in until the mixture resembles breadcrumbs. Stir in the grated cheese and thyme and mix well. Add the cold water and stir to bring everything together into a dough – if you prefer, you can do this in a food processor. Roll out the pastry and use it to line a 30cm tart tin, then prick the pastry all over with a fork. Leave it in the fridge to chill for about 30 minutes.

Preheat the oven to 200°C/Fan 180°C. Line the tin with baking parchment and fill it with baking beans or rice. Bake the pastry for about 15 minutes, then remove the paper and beans or rice and cook for another 5 minutes until golden brown.

In a large pan, melt the butter and cook the chopped chard stalks with the onion for 4–5 minutes. Add the chard leaves and cook for a further 4–5 minutes.

In a large bowl, beat the eggs and extra yolks with the cream and season with salt and plenty of black pepper. Stir in the chopped herbs and grated cheese.

Fill the pastry case with the greens and onion, then add the curd cheese or crumbled feta. Pour over the cream and egg mixture. Bake for 45–55 minutes until set, then allow to cool. Serve with a dressed green salad. *Recipe photographs overleaf.*

It may seem trite to include a mere omelette, but they are harder to make than you might think. Apart from anything else you need the right pan for a good omelette. I'm a bit of a purist, so I use a well-seasoned black De Buyer steel pan, 24cm in diameter. The amount of butter you start with is also very important – ten grams is the perfect amount; more makes the omelette too greasy. I've suggested adding cheese and chives which is a favourite filling of mine, but you can add mushrooms or indeed ham or crab if not vegetarian. As a regular guest on BBC One's *Saturday Kitchen*, I'm not sorry that some years ago they dropped the omelette challenge. It's nerve-wracking enough to do live television, but asking you to compete to cook the quickest omelette added another layer of stress. I remember I was once disqualified, as in my haste I forgot to whisk the eggs in a bowl and broke them straight into the frying pan.

CHEESE & CHIVE OMELETTE SERVES 1

10g butter
3 eggs, well beaten
30g strong vegetarian
　Cheddar cheese, grated
Chopped chives

Melt the butter in a 20–25cm non-stick frying pan and swirl it around the pan to coat the base. Add the beaten eggs and allow the pan to sit undisturbed for about 30 seconds, then gently start bringing in the uncooked egg from the edges to the centre of the pan.

When all the egg is softly set, sprinkle over the cheese and herbs. Then either flip one side of the omelette over the other to form a semicircle or roll the omelette, using a spatula or wooden spoon.

This is the sauce we use in our fish and chip shops. Some people, perhaps more used to sauce made with curry powder, find it a bit too exotic based as it is on a Goan masala, but most seem to like it.

STEIN'S CHIPS WITH CURRY SAUCE

MAKES 350–400ML OF SAUCE

Curry sauce
4 tbsp vegetable oil
30g Goan curry paste
    (see below)
2 medium onions, chopped
30g tomato paste
160g block of creamed
    coconut, chopped
1 tsp sea salt

Goan curry paste
35g red chillies
20g root ginger, grated
3½ tsp ground coriander
3 garlic cloves, roughly chopped
1 rounded tsp ground cumin
1 tbsp sunflower oil
1 tsp ground turmeric
½ tsp tamarind paste

Chips
550g medium-sized potatoes
    (Maris Pipers are good)
Groundnut, sunflower,
    vegetable or olive oil
    or goose fat
Salt

In a spice grinder or using a pestle and mortar, grind the curry paste ingredients until smooth. The paste can be stored in a glass jar in the fridge for up to a week.

For the curry sauce, heat a tablespoon of the oil in a pan, add the 30g of curry paste and fry for a minute until fragrant. Add the remaining oil and gently fry the chopped onions until softened, then add the tomato paste, creamed coconut, salt and 400ml of water. Stir to dissolve the coconut, then bring to a simmer and cook gently for 15–20 minutes. Blend to a smooth sauce in a blender or with a stick blender. You can freeze any leftover sauce for the next time you make chips. It's fine for up to 3 months.

For the chips, peel the potatoes and cut them to your desired shape. For thin chips, cut the potatoes into 1cm-thick slices and then lengthways into chips. For rough-cut chips, cut the potatoes into wedges. For goose fat chips, cut them into 1cm-thick slices and then lengthways into 2cm-wide, flatter chips. Quickly rinse the chips under cold water to remove the starch and dry them well.

I usually cook chips in groundnut oil as it's more stable at higher temperatures, but sunflower or vegetable oils are fine, too. Chips are also fantastic cooked in olive oil, but not extra virgin. For goose fat chips you will need to melt about 2 x 350g cans of goose fat in a medium-sized pan, so that you have a sufficient depth in which to cook the chips – the pan should not be more than one-third full.

To cook the chips, heat the oil or fat to 120°C. Drop a large handful of the chips into a chip basket and cook until they are tender when pierced with the tip of a knife but they've not taken on any colour – about 5 minutes. Lift out and drain, then cook the next batch.

To finish, heat the oil or fat to 190°C and cook the chips in batches until crisp and golden – about 2 minutes. Lift them on to kitchen paper, drain and then sprinkle with salt. Serve immediately.

This is a North Indian vegetarian street food dish that's made from dried white peas (vatana) and served with flatbreads called kulchas. I first tasted it on a recent trip to Old Delhi – my guide said it was the best dish in all of Delhi.

MATAR KULCHA SERVES 4

350g dried white peas or
   chickpeas, soaked overnight

Fried spices
1 tbsp vegetable oil
½ tsp cumin seeds
¼ tsp hot chilli powder
½ tsp chaat masala
1 tsp ground coriander

Jaljeera masala
Large handful of mint leaves,
   roughly chopped
1 tsp cumin seeds, toasted
½ tsp amchur (mango powder)
½–1 tsp salt
½ tsp asafoetida
1 tsp fennel seeds
1 tsp black peppercorns
1 tbsp seedless tamarind paste
1 tsp chilli flakes (or 2 dried
   Kashmiri chilies, broken up
1 black cardamom pod, seeds
   removed, husk discarded

Toppings
1 red onion, finely chopped
1 tomato, finely chopped
Small handful of coriander,
   leaves, roughly chopped
1 green chilli, cut into strips
10g root ginger, sliced into strips
1 lemon, cut into wedges

Kulchas
250g plain flour, plus extra
   for rolling out
½ tsp baking powder
¼ tsp bicarbonate of soda
½ tsp sugar
½–1 tsp salt
1 tbsp nigella seeds
4 tbsp thick natural yoghurt
1 tbsp oil or ghee, plus extra
   for brushing
100ml warm water

To make the kulchas, combine the dry ingredients in a large bowl, then add the yoghurt, oil or ghee and two-thirds of the water. Stir to bring together into a dough, adding more water as necessary.

Tip the dough on to a lightly floured surface and knead for about 8–10 minutes (or in a mixer with a dough hook for 3–4 minutes) until soft and smooth. Put the dough back in a clean bowl and cover with a clean damp tea towel, then leave to rest for about an hour.

Divide the dough into 8 pieces and roll each one into a ball. Roll each out to a disc about the size of a side plate (12–15cm).

Heat a large heavy frying pan. Brush one side of a kulcha with water and cook over a medium heat until bubbles have formed on the surface, then turn over until you see brown spots. Keep the kulcha warm and repeat with the remaining dough, then brush each one with melted butter or ghee.

For the matar, drain the white peas or chickpeas, put them in a pan with 700ml of water and cook for about 20–30 minutes until tender, depending on the age of your peas. Alternatively, you can cook them in a pressure cooker for 7–8 minutes.

For the fried spices, heat the oil in a frying pan and fry the cumin seeds for 30 seconds, then add the remaining spices and fry until fragrant. Set aside.

For the jaljeera masala, put all the ingredients in a spice grinder with 2 tablespoons of water and blitz to a smooth paste.

Add the fried spices and the jaljeera masala to the cooked peas, then stir well, adding a little more water if the mixture seems too thick or dry. If the peas are not broken down enough, use a potato masher to create a soft consistency with some whole peas remaining.

Warm everything through, then serve in warmed bowls, topped with onion, tomato, fresh coriander, chilli, ginger and lemon wedges. Serve with the warm kulchas.

AVANT-GARDE VEGAN

I guess what I object to about veganism is the political 'We're destroying the planet by rearing animals' approach. I've quietly enjoyed vegetarian, non-dairy cooking in such countries as India and Sri Lanka for many years, and until people started loudly proclaiming this food as being vegan I never really noticed the difference. So, when I was due to meet Gaz Oakley – a successful chef who describes himself as an 'avant-garde vegan' and has 1.5 million followers on YouTube – when filming my *Food Stories* series, I was thinking I was going to have to work hard to show interest. But, at the same time, I was intrigued by Gaz's enormous social media following.

My experience with Gaz only goes to show that it's a great mistake to dismiss the enthusiasms of a much younger generation on the grounds perhaps of, 'I've seen it all before', or 'What do they know?' Gaz has worked as a professional chef, but now he's focused on growing and cooking his own produce and sharing his expertise and recipes online. What I found in him was a wonderful enthusiasm for his vegetables, his garden and the view over the hills of Monmouthshire beyond it. I love the fact that he is excited about getting up in the morning to see how well his strawberries are growing or to marvel at his pumpkins.

Following him through his colourful and well thought-out vegetable garden reminded me of my own enthusiasm about gardening in the sandy soil of our house on Trevose Head in Cornwall. I remember the thrill of growing my first runner beans and sweet peas, as well as herbs such as lovage and a curious one called coriander that I couldn't believe anyone could enjoy. In fact, my very first book, *English Seafood Cookery*, contained delightful illustrations by an artist called Katinka Kew who came over to my garden and made a little sketch of me between the French beans and the leeks. I've still got the drawing.

Meeting Gaz and responding to his energy and passion for great produce and food put me in mind of a song by Barclay James Harvest called 'Galadriel' and the refrain running right through it: 'Oh, what it is to be young'. Even so, I have to admit that when Gaz announced he was going to cook a vegetable-based pizza topped with a sauce made with rhubarb from his garden, I thought to myself: this won't work.

But then I started watching what he was doing, and it was clear that his earlier classical training as a chef was paying off. He was fully aware of the importance of plenty of umami flavour in the pizza, which he achieved with a sauce of leek, miso paste, nutritional yeast

'My experience with Gaz only goes to show that it's a great mistake to dismiss the enthusiasms of a much younger generation on the grounds perhaps of, "I've seen it all before" or "What do they know?"'

and beer. This rarebit sauce was good but a bit more complicated than the mozzarella topping on our pizza margherita. You can find a slightly simplified version of Gaz's pizza on page 127.

I started watching Gaz on YouTube and on TikTok, where he also has a substantial following, and I can see from his example why young people get most of their cooking inspiration from social media. Gaz is just very watchable. He has a calm enthusiasm and the dishes he makes are colourful and well filmed. Because of his training he really knows what he's doing. A lot of people think the idea of going into restaurant cooking is too hard, with long antisocial hours, but my gosh, how it has paid off for Gaz.

This book is not only about recipes but also about where we are with cooking today in this country. I've realised how important it is to take notice of the wealth of new food knowledge on social media channels, such as Instagram, TikTok and YouTube, and embrace it. In the end, what matters is that you know how to cook flavourful food, vegan or not.

The plethora of toppings for pizza leads to evermore decision making. Do I go for 'nduja, pepperoni, mushrooms, Hawaiian or even a tomato-free bianco or perhaps quattro formaggi? In the end, I'm ashamed to say, I generally opt for a margherita, simply because it's about a crisp base, a great tomato sauce and mozzarella, combined with memories of the first genuinely fabulous pizza I ever had – yes, I would say that wouldn't I? It was on a street in Naples with David Pritchard, the director I worked with for so many years, prior to a filming trip to the island of Procida. Of course, there needs to be basil as well to complete the colours of the Italian flag. By the way, the sauce recipe will make more than you need for the pizzas, but you can freeze any that's left for another dish or more pizzas. Check that your mozzarella is suitable for vegetarians.

PIZZA MARGHERITA MAKES 4 PIZZAS

Dough
500g strong plain white bread
    flour, plus extra for dusting
7g sachet of fast-action
    dried yeast
½ tsp sugar
10g salt
275ml lukewarm water
60ml olive oil, plus extra
    for greasing

Tomato sauce
6 tbsp extra virgin olive oil
4 fat garlic cloves, finely chopped
2 x 400g tins of plum tomatoes
Salt and black pepper

Topping
2 x 150g mozzarella balls, sliced
Good handful of fresh
    basil leaves
30g vegetarian Parmesan-style
    cheese, freshly grated
    (optional)

Start by making the dough. Sift the flour into a large bowl and add the yeast, sugar and salt. Make a well in the centre, add the water and oil and bring everything together with your hands into a rough dough.

Dust your work surface with flour and knead the dough for about 5 minutes until it is smooth and elastic. Transfer it to a bowl lightly greased with olive oil. Cover with a tea towel and leave the dough in a warm place to rise for 30–60 minutes until doubled in bulk.

While the dough is rising, make the tomato sauce. Heat the oil in a saucepan with the garlic. Once it starts to sizzle, add the tinned tomatoes and simmer for about 20 minutes, breaking them up with a wooden spoon as they cook. Season with salt and plenty of pepper. If the sauce seems a bit thin, allow it to reduce down a little more until thickened and pulpy so it doesn't run off the pizza. Whizz the sauce with a stick blender until fairly smooth.

Preheat the oven to 230°C/Fan 210°C. If you have a pizza stone, put it in the oven to heat up. Otherwise, preheat your baking sheets.

Divide the dough into 4 pieces. On a lightly floured board, roll out each piece with a rolling pin into a circle 3–4mm thick. Transfer each circle to a sheet of baking parchment. Top each base with 3–4 tablespoons of tomato sauce and some slices of mozzarella. Season with salt and pepper and lift the pizzas, with the parchment, on to your pizza stone or baking sheet. You'll probably find it best to cook the pizzas a couple at a time.

Cook in the preheated oven for 7–10 minutes until crisp. Scatter over the basil leaves, season with more black pepper if you like and sprinkle with grated cheese, if using.

As the main ingredient in a big main course or as a dish on a buffet, squash has the advantage of being very colourful, especially if slightly charred. I've suggested peeling the squash but it's often easier to leave the peel on, unless it is very thick. I use yoghurt in the dressing, but if you'd like to make this a vegan dish, you could replace the yoghurt with olive oil.

ROAST BUTTERNUT SQUASH WITH BULGUR & LENTIL SALAD SERVES 6

Squash
800g–1kg butternut squash, peeled, deseeded and sliced into 1.5cm thick wedges
3 tbsp olive oil
3–4 tsp harissa paste
Salt and black pepper

Salad
200g bulgur wheat
250g cooked green or puy lentils (from a pouch or tin)
45g flatleaf parsley, chopped
15g mint or coriander
½ red onion, finely chopped
75g dried apricots, finely chopped
40g pistachios, chopped
3 tbsp olive oil
1 tbsp pomegranate molasses

Dressing
4 tbsp natural yoghurt
1 tsp lemon juice
1 garlic clove, grated

To garnish
Flatleaf parsley, roughly chopped
Toasted sesame seeds

Preheat the oven to 200°C/Fan 180°C. Put the wedges of butternut squash in a roasting tin, add the olive oil and harissa and toss to coat. Season with salt and pepper. Roast the squash for 25–35 minutes or until tender and slightly browned at the edges.

Bring a pan of water to the boil, add the bulgur wheat and cook for 10 minutes. Drain in a sieve, then cool under cold running water and drain again. Mix with the other salad ingredients in a large bowl and toss to combine. Season with salt and pepper. Mix the dressing ingredients in a jug and season with a good pinch of salt.

Serve the wedges of butternut squash on a bed of the bulgur wheat and lentil salad. Drizzle over the yoghurt dressing and scatter over the parsley leaves and sesame seeds.

I once got hauled over the coals by the old Kernow Society for daring to sell steak pasties made with puff pastry in my deli in Padstow. They described it as culinary appropriation, pointing out that I wasn't Cornish. Much as I love a Cornish pasty made with a lean shortcrust to ensure it doesn't break up, I do think that puff pastry is fabulous. Interestingly, I was also out of order in that we made our pasties with a top crimp, not a side one. Top crimp are Devon pasties, not Cornish. A French friend observed once that my pasties looked like dinosaurs, but whatever the shape, the combination here is really very pleasant.

STRONG CHEDDAR & POTATO PUFF PASTRY PASTIES MAKES 4

20g butter or 2 tbsp oil
1 onion or 1 leek, chopped
230g floury potatoes, such as Maris Pipers, peeled and cut into 1.5cm dice
150g vintage or extra-mature vegetarian Cheddar (or other flavourful cheese)
Small handful of parsley, chopped
Flour, for dusting
500g block of puff pastry
1 egg, beaten
Salt and black pepper

Start by making the filling. Heat the butter or oil in a pan, add the onion or leek and the diced potatoes and fry gently over a medium heat for 10–15 minutes until softened. If they start to catch, add a tablespoon or so of water. Season with a little salt and plenty of pepper, then transfer to a bowl and allow to cool completely. Stir in the grated cheese and the parsley.

On a lightly floured surface, roll out the pastry to a thickness of about 3–4mm. Cut out 4 discs of pastry about 15–17cm in diameter. Use a small side plate to cut around if that helps. Line a baking sheet with baking parchment.

Divide the cooled filling between the 4 pastry discs, placing it to one side of the circle and leaving a border of 2cm around the edge. Brush the border with a little beaten egg, then fold half the pastry over the filling to form a semicircle. Seal the edges and crimp firmly with the tines of a fork to prevent the filling escaping.

Transfer the pasties to the lined baking sheet and chill for about 30 minutes or longer – you can make them to this stage up to a day before cooking.

Preheat the oven to 200°C/Fan 180°C. Brush the chilled pasties with beaten egg and bake for about 25 minutes until golden and crisp. Allow to cool for 10 minutes or so before eating.

It's not that this particular dish is a national favourite, but traybakes certainly are much loved. So enamoured am I of Greek peppers or tomatoes stuffed with rice that I have adapted the idea to a traybake, simply because it's so easy to do. I've swapped the rice for pearl barley, as I love its al dente texture, and I've included some finely chopped roasted red pepper, along with garlic, onion, oregano and cayenne. I like to serve this with a simple green salad.

TRAYBAKE OF STUFFED PEPPERS WITH PEARL BARLEY, FETA & OREGANO SERVES 4

3 tbsp olive oil, plus extra
    for brushing the peppers
1 onion, finely chopped
2 garlic cloves, finely chopped
250g pearl barley
¼ tsp cayenne pepper
½ tsp dried oregano
2 tomatoes, chopped
750ml vegetable or
    chicken stock
1 roasted red pepper,
    finely chopped
50g pitted olives, black
    or green, chopped
About 50g flatleaf parsley,
    chopped
4 large bell peppers, red,
    orange or yellow
12 cherry tomatoes
75g vegetarian feta cheese,
    crumbled
2 tbsp toasted pine nuts
Salt and black pepper

Heat the olive oil in a pan over a medium heat and add the onion and garlic. Fry gently until softened, then add the pearl barley, cayenne, oregano, chopped tomatoes and stock. Put a lid on the pan – a little askew so there's a gap for steam to escape – and cook for about 25 minutes until the barley is just tender and the stock has been absorbed. Taste and season with salt and pepper. Stir in the chopped roasted red pepper, olives and most of the parsley – reserve a tablespoon for garnish.

Preheat the oven to 180°C/Fan 160°C. Cut the bell peppers in half through the middle, leaving the stem intact if possible. Scrape out the seeds. Brush inside and out with a little olive oil and place them on a baking tray.

Divide the pearl barley mixture between the peppers, then add the cherry tomatoes to the tray and cover the whole tray with foil. Bake for about 40 minutes until the peppers are soft. Remove the foil and sprinkle over the feta, then put the tray back in the oven for about 5 minutes, uncovered, to heat the cheese through.

Sprinkle the peppers with parsley and the pine nuts and serve warm or at room temperature with a dressed green salad.

I really liked Gaz Oakley who we filmed with for my *Food Stories* series, and I enjoyed his plant-based pizza. I have to say it's quite a bit of work, but it's fascinating to give it a try.

WELSH GARDEN PIZZA

MAKES 2 LARGE DEEP-PAN PIZZAS (OR 4 THINNER ONES)

Pizza dough
590g strong white bread flour, plus extra for dusting
7g sachet of fast-action dried yeast
10g fine sea salt
325ml lukewarm water
3 tbsp olive oil

Rhubarb ketchup
2–3 tbsp oil
1 onion, finely chopped
4 garlic cloves, finely chopped
1 tsp ground cumin
1 tsp ground coriander
1 tsp celery salt
2 tsp smoked paprika (pimentón)
400g rhubarb, thinly sliced
60g brown soft sugar
1 tbsp fresh or dried sage
1 tbsp fresh or dried thyme
2 bay leaves
1 tbsp miso paste
3 tbsp tomato paste
400g tin of chopped tomatoes
125ml white wine vinegar

Rarebit sauce
1 leek, finely sliced
1 large garlic clove, chopped
55g non-dairy butter
30g plain flour
125ml beer (preferably Welsh)
125ml non-dairy milk
1 tsp Dijon mustard
2 tsp miso paste
15g nutritional yeast
Squeeze of lemon juice
Sea salt and ground white pepper

Topping ideas
Roasted carrots and/or beetroots
Fresh herbs, roughly chopped

Start by making the dough. Sift the flour into a large bowl and add the yeast and salt. Make a well in the centre, add the water and olive oil, then bring everything together with your hands into a rough dough. Dust a work surface with flour and knead the dough for about 5 minutes until it is smooth and elastic. Transfer to a bowl lightly oiled with olive oil. Cover with a clean tea towel and leave in a warm place to rise for 30–60 minutes until doubled in bulk.

Next make the rhubarb ketchup. Heat the oil in a large pan and gently fry the onion and garlic until softened. Add the cumin, coriander, celery salt and smoked paprika and fry for a minute, then add the rhubarb, sugar, sage, thyme, bay leaves, miso, tomato paste, tinned tomatoes and white wine vinegar. Bring to the boil and simmer over a medium heat until the rhubarb and tomatoes have broken down, stirring occasionally to prevent the mixture catching on the bottom of the pan. Cook for about 20 minutes until thick and glossy, then set aside to cool.

For the rarebit sauce, fry the leek and garlic very gently in the non-dairy butter until soft, then add the flour and stir to form a roux. Stir in the beer, non-dairy milk, mustard, miso and nutritional yeast and season with salt and white pepper. Cook over a medium heat, stirring frequently until the mixture comes to the boil and is thick and bubbling. Taste and season with a little lemon juice, then set aside until ready to assemble your pizza.

Preheat your oven to 230°C/Fan 210°C or as high as it will go and preheat 2 baking trays or pizza stones. (Alternatively, use a pizza oven if you have one.) Tip the dough on to a lightly floured surface and lightly knead. Divide it into 2 (or 4) balls and roll each ball into a disc about 25–30cm in diameter. Do this on a sheet of baking parchment to allow easy transfer to your preheated trays. Set aside for about 10 minutes.

Top each pizza with some of the rhubarb ketchup, add some roasted vegetables, then spoon over the rarebit sauce. Transfer to the hot baking trays or stones and bake for 7–10 minutes until cooked and golden and charred in places. Top with herbs and serve immediately.

CHICKEN & DUCK

I first tried brining a bird before roasting with a Christmas turkey a couple of years ago. The results were so special that I've adapted the recipe for chicken, which is far easier to cope with (see page 153). The problem with the turkey was finding a pan big enough to immerse the twenty-pound bird and I ended up borrowing a stock pot from my Seafood Restaurant. The science of brining meat is that the water content is replaced with salt by osmosis, thus concentrating the flavour. If you use a light brine solution like the one in my recipe, the meat doesn't become noticeably salty like ham, but the subtle presence of salt right through the flesh enhances the taste. It's very noticeable, I think, how many of the nation's favourite dishes are based on chicken. Of course, this has something to do with its price and ability to take on other flavours, but actually I do think it's worth spending a bit more money and getting free-range chicken, simply because the extra flavour makes the dishes so much more enjoyable. This is not only the case for classics such as roast chicken and chicken, ham and leek puff pastry pie but also with spicy dishes, such as my chipotle chicken burrito, jerk chicken and Korean fried chicken wings.

During a rather moving visit to a Ukrainian restaurant in South Kensington in London, I happened to notice chicken kyiv on the menu. The origins of the recipe are obscure – it could be French, it could be Russian or most likely it came from the Continental Hotel in the Ukrainian capital. In view of the terrible things that have been happening there, as far as I am concerned this dish always came from Kyiv. It became popular in this country when launched by M&S as one of their first ready meals in 1979. It's one of those dishes that everybody loves because of the way the garlic and parsley butter oozes out of the crisp breadcrumbs as you cut into the chicken.

CHICKEN KYIV SERVES 4

125g salted butter,
   at room temperature
10g dill, chopped
10g parsley, chopped
2 garlic cloves, very finely
   chopped or grated
4 chicken breasts with wing
   bone attached, skinned
125g flour
2 eggs, beaten
200g panko breadcrumbs
6–8 tbsp vegetable oil,
   for frying
Salt and black pepper

To serve
Mashed potatoes

Put the butter in a bowl, add the dill, parsley and garlic, then season well with salt and pepper and mix thoroughly. Wrap the butter in cling film or baking parchment and roll it into a sausage shape, then chill it in the freezer until completely solidified.

Preheat the oven to 180°C/Fan 160°C. Starting at the fatter end of a chicken breast, cut a slit horizontally through the breast to form a pocket. Be careful not to cut all the way through or the butter will leak out. Repeat with the remaining chicken breasts.

Cut the roll of chilled butter into 8 slices and slip 2 of these slices into each slit. Close the pocket in each breast and press down a little to prevent the butter escaping.

Put the flour, beaten eggs and breadcrumbs in separate bowls. Carefully dip each piece of chicken in flour, shake off the excess, then dip it into the egg and finally the breadcrumbs. Then dip each piece just into the beaten egg and breadcrumbs, so the chicken has a double coating.

Heat the oil in a frying pan and add 2 of the chicken breasts and gently fry until golden on both sides. Cook the remaining breasts in the same way, then transfer them all to the oven and cook for 15–20 minutes until cooked through – the chicken should be at least 70°C when probed at the thickest part.

Drain the cooked chicken on kitchen paper to remove any excess oil. Mash is a perfect accompaniment.

This is without question one of the nation's favourite dishes. To me, it's a bit like sticky toffee pudding in that you look up and down a menu and you know what you'd really like, but you feel a little shame-faced about ordering it because everyone knows you have it every time. At its best, this dish is a combination of tandoori chicken with a rich spicy tomato sauce cooked in ghee or butter. It's often said to have been invented in the UK, and indeed it is one of those dishes which is as much British as Indian, but I've tasted a very similar dish called murgh makhani in Amritsar in Punjab.

CHICKEN TIKKA MASALA SERVES 4

2 tsp cumin seeds
1½ tsp coriander seeds
750g skinless, boneless chicken
   breast meat (about 4 breasts)
25g ghee or clarified
   butter, melted
1½ tbsp lemon juice
Small handful of coriander
   leaves, roughly chopped,
   plus extra to garnish

Marinade
Seeds from 12 green
   cardamom pods, crushed
Juice of 1 large lemon
1 tsp Kashmiri chilli powder
1 tsp ground turmeric
1 tsp salt
150ml natural yoghurt
25g root ginger, grated
2 garlic cloves, grated

Sauce
3 tbsp ghee, clarified butter
   or vegetable oil
1 large onion, finely sliced
2 garlic cloves, grated
25g root ginger, grated
½ tsp Kashmiri chilli powder
1 tsp garam masala
225g chopped tomatoes,
   tinned or fresh
1 tbsp tomato paste
1 tbsp ground almonds
½ tsp salt
1 tsp sugar
120ml double cream
3 green chillies, slit open

To serve
Chapatis (see p.264)
Pilau rice (see p.264)
Lemon wedges

Toast the cumin and coriander seeds in a dry frying pan until fragrant. Grind them in a spice grinder or with a pestle and mortar.

Put a teaspoon of the toasted and ground seeds in a bowl with the remaining ingredients for the marinade. Cut the chicken into 3–4cm chunks, add them to the bowl, then toss to coat. Set aside to marinate for about half an hour.

Line your grill pan with foil and preheat the grill to high. Take the chicken pieces out of the marinade and brush them with melted ghee or clarified butter. Cook the chicken under the grill – or on a barbecue – for 5–6 minutes on each side until lightly charred in places and cooked through.

For the sauce, heat the 3 tablespoons of ghee, clarified butter or oil in a pan and fry the onion until soft and golden. Add the grated garlic and ginger and cook for a few minutes. Stir in the remaining toasted seeds and the other sauce spices and cook for 1–2 minutes. Add the tomatoes, tomato paste, ground almonds, salt and 300ml of water, then bring to the boil and simmer for 10 minutes. Add any remaining marinade together with the sugar, cream and green chillies to the sauce and simmer gently for 10 minutes until it has thickened a little.

Add the chicken to the sauce and cook for a few more minutes, then stir in the lemon juice and coriander. Garnish with more coriander leaves, then serve with some chapatis, pilau rice and lemon wedges.

The Central American version of fermented vegetables, similar to kimchi and sauerkraut, is a white cabbage, carrot and onion mix flavoured with coriander and called curtido. I spent a really interesting afternoon in Somerset recently, testing a whole range of ferments with Peter Prescott, who used to be in partnership with Terence Conran running the Boundary restaurant in Shoreditch. Now he concentrates on what I mistakenly kept calling pickles but ferments they are. To celebrate the curtido, which I found particularly exciting, I've written a recipe for a flour tortilla burrito with chicken, chipotles in adobo, black beans and Lancashire cheese. Peter's curtido is available online (www.cultjar.co.uk) but I find that kimchi works very well too. The sour, crunchy ferment really complements the rest of the ingredients.

CHIPOTLE CHICKEN BURRITO MAKES 4

2 boneless chicken breasts,
    skin on
Vegetable oil
30g lard
1 onion, chopped
1 large garlic clove, chopped
½ tsp dried oregano
400g tin of black or kidney
    beans, drained and rinsed
4 large flour tortillas
Handful of finely shredded
    cabbage or lettuce
1 ripe avocado, sliced
2 tbsp chipotles in adobo sauce
    (shop-bought or see p.268)
4 tsp soured cream
2 tomatoes, sliced or chopped
Small handful of fresh coriander,
    roughly chopped
70g Lancashire cheese,
    crumbled
4 tbsp curtido or kimchi
Salt and black pepper

To serve
Soured cream
Curtido or kimchi

Preheat a barbecue or a griddle pan. Brush the chicken with a little oil and season well with salt and pepper (or with Rick's peppermix, see page 270). Grill the chicken until cooked through – the internal temperature at the thickest part should be at least 70°C. Keep the chicken warm.

While the chicken is cooking, heat the lard in a frying pan and fry the onion and garlic until softened. Stir in the oregano, then add the black or kidney beans and warm them through thoroughly. Season with salt and pepper, then roughly mash the beans with the back of a wooden spoon or potato masher. Set aside the bean mixture to keep warm.

Briefly soften the tortillas on the barbecue or griddle to make them pliable or warm them in a microwave.

Cut the chicken into slices 3–4mm thick. To assemble the burrito, lay the warm tortillas out on a work surface. Divide the bean mix, cabbage or lettuce, chicken slices, avocado, chipotles in adobo sauce, soured cream, tomatoes and coriander between the tortillas, placing the ingredients on the half nearest you. Top with crumbled cheese and curtido or kimchi. Fold in the sides, then fold up the bottom and roll tightly tucking the sides in.

Cut each burrito in half at an angle and serve with extra soured cream and curtido or kimchi.

This is not Chinese food. It's a dish firmly based in these islands, much influenced by Chinese food. Indeed, a lot of the early Indian and Bangladeshi dishes in this country were a local take, using what you could get before authentic ingredients from the country of origin became available. But if something tastes delicious, as this does, there's no suggestion that it's second rate, just an example of how food is constantly changing and evolving.

CHINESE CHICKEN CURRY SERVES 4

500g skinless chicken breast
    or thigh meat, cut into
    3cm cubes
2 tsp cornflour
1 tbsp soy sauce
1½ tbsp vegetable oil
1 large onion, cut into
    large dice
60g chestnut mushrooms,
    sliced
1½ tbsp medium curry powder
1 tsp ground turmeric
300ml chicken stock
1½ tsp honey
1 level tbsp cornflour mixed
    with 2–3 tbsp water
100g frozen peas
2 spring onions, sliced on
    the diagonal, to garnish

To serve
Egg-fried rice (see p.263)

Put the chicken in a bowl and mix with the cornflour and soy sauce until coated.

Heat the oil in a wok, add the chicken and stir-fry for a few minutes. Add the onion and mushrooms, then the curry powder and turmeric and cook for a minute. Add the chicken stock, honey and cornflour mix and cook for 3–4 minutes. Add the peas and cook for another 2 minutes until everything has heated through.

Taste and add a dash more soy sauce or a pinch of salt if required. Garnish with the spring onions and serve with egg-fried rice.

A classic that originated in Middlesbrough, this high-calorie, post-pub, takeaway food is beloved in the Teeside area. It can be deep-fried, shallow-fried or air-fried and is served with chips or salad. The late and much-lamented Hairy Biker, Dave Myers, described this as being a heart attack on a plate. But sometimes that's just the sort of food you want.

CHICKEN PARMO SERVES 2

2 chicken breasts
   (each 150–160g)
2 tbsp plain flour
1 large egg, beaten
100g panko breadcrumbs
Sunflower oil, for frying
85g Cheddar, Red Leicester
   or a mixture, grated
Salt and black pepper

Béchamel sauce
25g butter
25g plain flour
250ml milk
1 bay leaf

First make the béchamel. Melt the butter in a pan and stir in the flour to make a roux. Cook for a minute over a medium heat, then gradually whisk in the milk, add the bay leaf and season with salt and pepper. Stir with a wooden spoon until the sauce comes to the boil and thickens, then set it aside.

Cut a chicken breast horizontally through the middle and open it up like a book. Place it between 2 sheets of parchment paper and bash it with a rolling pin until it is about 6–7mm thick. Repeat with the other chicken breast.

Put the flour, egg and breadcrumbs on 3 separate plates. Season the chicken breasts with salt and pepper and dust them all over with flour. Dip each one in beaten egg, allow any excess to drip off, then dredge in the breadcrumbs. Heat the oil in a large frying pan and fry the chicken breasts for about 4 minutes on each side until crisp, golden and cooked through.

Meanwhile, preheat the grill to medium-high. Put the chicken breasts on a baking sheet and top each one with béchamel and grated cheese. Grill until golden and bubbling, then season with freshly ground black pepper. Serve immediately, perhaps with chips or a big green salad.

You can find chicken katsu in Wagamama, Yo! Sushi and Itsu as well as in supermarket chiller cabinets, testimony to the dish's popularity in this country. There are probably very few people under the age of 30 who don't know it. It's a dish that combines the Japanese love of protein fried in panko breadcrumbs with the flavours of India. Personally, being perhaps more familiar with the flavours of India than many Japanese, I prefer my katsu a little bit hotter than usual, so have added a modest amount of cayenne pepper to the recipe and I like a splash of vinegar to give it a bit more vigour. Katsu curry often appears on vegetarian menus, and I think slices of aubergine are the perfect alternative to chicken.

CHICKEN KATSU CURRY SERVES 4

4 small chicken breasts
    (or 2 aubergines,
    thickly sliced)
2 tbsp plain flour
1 large egg, beaten
60–70g panko breadcrumbs
60ml sunflower
    or vegetable oil
Salt and black pepper

Rice
400g sushi rice
½ tsp salt

Katsu sauce
2 tbsp oil
2 carrots, chopped
1 large onion, chopped
2 garlic cloves, chopped
10g root ginger, grated
1 tbsp medium curry powder
½ tsp cayenne pepper
400ml tin of coconut milk
150ml chicken stock
2–3 tsp soy sauce
2 tsp honey
2 tbsp malt vinegar

To serve
Steamed green beans
    or tenderstem broccoli

Wash the sushi rice until it runs clear, then leave it to soak for about 30 minutes in cold water.

For the sauce, heat the oil in a pan and gently fry the carrots, onion, garlic and ginger until soft. Add the curry powder and cayenne and cook for a minute, then add the coconut milk, chicken stock, soy sauce, honey and the vinegar. Simmer for 20–25 minutes until the vegetables are really soft and the liquid has reduced a little. Using a stick blender or liquidiser, blitz to form a smooth sauce, then taste and add a little more soy sauce or honey if needed.

Place a chicken breast between 2 sheets of cling film or baking parchment and bash it into an escalope about 3–4mm thick. Season with salt and pepper. Repeat with the other breasts. Put the flour, beaten egg and breadcrumbs on 3 separate plates. Dip each chicken breast in flour, then egg and finally the breadcrumbs. If using slices of aubergine, you don't need to bash them, just season and coat them in the same way as the chicken.

Put the soaked rice in a pan with 500ml of cold water and the salt, cover with a lid and bring to the boil. Once boiling, immediately turn the heat down to a simmer and cook for 10 minutes. Turn off the heat, leave the lid on the pan and allow the rice to steam for a further 10 minutes.

Heat the oil in a large frying pan and fry the chicken, or aubergine, for 4–5 minutes on each side until golden. Transfer to a warm plate lined with kitchen paper and keep warm if cooking in batches.

Slice each chicken breast or aubergine slice on the diagonal into 5 pieces. Spoon some rice into a teacup and compress, then turn out on to a plate to make a rice dome. Add slices of chicken or aubergine and spoon over some of the sauce. Serve with green vegetables.

This classic of Tex-Mex cuisine has really caught on over here. Fajitas were originally made with grilled skirt steak – the term 'fajitas' means 'strips of meat' – but are much more likely to be made with chicken these days. It's interesting that this recipe calls for garlic powder in addition to all the other flavourings. Purists, and I have to say I count myself among them, would usually eschew garlic powder in favour of fresh and crushed, but actually it's a fabulous condiment in some American dishes. I particularly love it in ranch dressing.

CHICKEN FAJITAS SERVES 4

About 450g skinless, boneless
  chicken thigh or breast meat
½ tsp hot chilli powder
1 tsp ground cumin
½ tsp ground coriander
1 tsp garlic powder
1 tsp smoked paprika
  (pimentón)
½ tsp salt
1 tsp dried oregano
2 tbsp vegetable oil
1 onion, finely sliced
1 red pepper, deseeded
  and sliced into thin strips
1 yellow pepper deseeded
  and sliced into thin strips
½ lime
4 large flour tortillas

Toppings (optional)
Pico de gallo salsa (see p.268)
Sliced onions and tomatoes
4 tbsp soured cream
1 avocado, stoned and sliced
Handful of fresh
  coriander leaves
Lime wedges

To serve
Sweet potato wedges
  (see p.260)

Cut the chicken into finger-sized strips and put them in a bowl. Add the spices, salt and oregano, toss to coat the chicken in all the flavourings, then set aside for 10–15 minutes.

Heat the oil in a large wide frying pan and when it's hot, add the chicken and stir-fry for a couple of minutes. Add the onion and peppers and continue to cook for another 4–5 minutes. Take the pan off the heat and squeeze the lime juice over the contents.

Meanwhile, warm the tortillas in a dry pan for about 10 seconds on each side or in a microwave.

Divide the chicken and pepper mixture between the warmed tortillas. Add whichever toppings you like, fold up and serve immediately with sweet potato wedges.

HOURIA CAFÉ, BRISTOL

Being from the West Country, I've always regarded Bristol as being just another local city. Plymouth, too, I always think of as a slightly rough garrison town but still one of us. They all speak a bit like us and therefore probably have the same West Country attributes. Bristol is a bit further away from Cornwall than Plymouth and a lot further away in that it was the historical centre of the slavery trade in this country. Now it is a city with a huge cultural diversity where more than seventy different languages are spoken.

On my previous visit I went to a community centre in the inner city area of Easton where they were teaching teenage single mothers how to cook. And this time, I went to a local community café employing women who have been victims of modern slavery. The visit reinforced for me how food really does bring us all together, wherever you are in the world.

The café is called Houria, which means 'freedom' in Arabic. I was introduced to the café's inspiration and founder, Kimberly Prado, known as Kim, who explained that the café is about empowering women survivors to achieve their dreams through food. She is passionate about the healing power of food and the café seeks to provide free training, safe employment and a sense of belonging in a community of women in Bristol. I've been told that these women have suffered the most harrowing experiences and one of Kim's aims is to increase awareness of the huge problem of modern slavery but through food and flavour.

On the day we were filming, three women were preparing much-loved dishes from home – dishes that they had learned from their mothers, no recipes needed. An Egyptian woman, Amel, cooked a dish of rice, chickpeas, lentils and pasta called koshari, which she says is comfort food and the national dish of Egypt. Mariam, from Pakistan, cooked a chicken pilau, something she would make twice a week back home, while Kim herself, who was born in the UK but is of Cape Verde heritage, cooked salt cod fishcakes. I thoroughly enjoyed it all as we sat and chatted over lunch.

In the short time we filmed at Houria it was plain to see the joy and confidence that cooking their familiar food brought out in these women. Amel spoke of the sense of peace, safety and family that working at Houria gave her, saying it made her feel: 'I can do it. I can do it'. To me, all those people, rescued from terrible circumstances, seemed to regain their joyful personalities just by their cooking.

'The visit reinforced for me how food really does bring us all together, wherever you are in the world.'

I remember talking to camera outside as we left the café about how much the experience had meant to me because I could see that the transformation of these women could lead to so much more for them and that is precisely what Kim's aims are. It's not just about working in the café, it's also about restoring self-esteem, allowing the women to blossom and gain in confidence and hopefully move out into the wider world and rebuild their lives. Houria also runs supper clubs and pop-up community feasts. They also have an outside catering service and even do takeaway feasts to enjoy at home. Bristolians are lucky enough to be able to have such things as aubergine and peanut curry or okra and tomato stew delivered to their door on a Friday night.

For me, the simple point that Kim has realised is that all these women have talents and skills because they learned how to cook from their mothers and grandmothers. My abiding memory is being in the kitchen with them as they cooked, lots of very normal gossip and chat – as would happen in any kitchen anywhere in the world; testament to the power of simply cooking and sharing good food.

This is inspired by the chicken at Gullus Kitchen in Fishponds, Bristol, where we filmed for my *Food Stories* series. Their recipe is more complex, so you'll have to go there for the real deal, but I've kept the essential flavourings of spring onions, scotch bonnet chillies, thyme and allspice. Scotch bonnets are the authentic chillies, but they are hot. I do think their flavour is important, though, so I suggest removing the seeds from some of them if you don't want your chicken very hot indeed. Jerk chicken is traditionally cooked in a jerk pan made out of an oil drum sawn in half and, in the Caribbean, over pimento wood, but I use my barbecue. Actually, the chicken is so good I would cook it in the oven if I had nothing else. The rice and peas are cooked in coconut milk and complement the spicy chicken beautifully. One tip, I skin the chicken for this dish as I find the marinade then penetrates better.

JERK CHICKEN WITH RICE & PEAS SERVES 6

1.5kg chicken thighs and
    drumsticks, skinned

Marinade
1 bunch of spring onions,
    chopped
3 fresh scotch bonnet chillies,
    chopped (seeds removed from
    2 unless you like lots of heat)
30g root ginger, chopped
6 large garlic cloves, sliced
3 tbsp vegetable oil
75ml malt or cider vinegar
2 tbsp soy sauce
Juice of 1 lime
1 tsp smoked paprika
1 tsp ground nutmeg
1 tbsp ground allspice
8 thyme sprigs, leaves stripped
    from the stalks
1 tbsp brown soft sugar

Rice and peas
400g long-grain white rice
400g tin of kidney beans,
    drained and rinsed
1 garlic clove, chopped
2 spring onions thinly sliced
3 thyme sprigs, leaves stripped
    from the stalks
150ml coconut milk
Salt

To serve
Mango and tomato salad
    (see p.262)

Put all the marinade ingredients into a blender or food processor and blend until smooth and brown. Pour the marinade into a bowl, add the pieces of chicken and turn them to coat. Cover the bowl and leave the chicken to marinate for 4 hours or longer in the fridge.

Light your barbecue. When it's hot and the coals are white, cook the chicken for 30–35 minutes, turning it every 6–10 minutes to ensure even cooking and browning. Use a temperature probe, if you have one, to check the chicken is cooked – it should be 70°C at the centre, but try not to let it get any hotter.

While the chicken is cooking, prepare the rice and peas. Put the rice in a pan with the kidney beans, garlic, spring onions, thyme, coconut milk, 350ml of water and a teaspoon of salt. Bring to the boil, then immediately turn down to a simmer, cover with a lid and cook for 12 minutes. Turn off the heat and leave the rice to steam, covered, for a further 5 minutes. Fluff it up with a fork and it's ready to serve.

Serve the chicken with the rice and salad.

I'm amazed at how quickly Korean food has become popular in this country. It's easy to see why, though, as it is sweet, spicy and full of interesting flavours like kimchi and gochujang chilli paste. There's a very good restaurant in New Malden called Cah Chi that I particularly like – the food critic Grace Dent described it as: 'an umami-drenched patch of extreme deliciousness' – and these chicken wings are the sort of thing you might find on their menu. Incidentally, New Malden is the biggest settlement of South Koreans in Europe and it also happens to be the largest North Korean diaspora outside the Korean peninsula, about 700 people at the last count. That's pretty special.

KOREAN FRIED CHICKEN WINGS WITH SOY, GARLIC, GINGER & GOCHUJANG SERVES 4 OR 8 AS A STARTER

15g root ginger, grated
75g cornflour
1kg chicken wings
1 litre vegetable oil
Salt and black pepper

Sauce
6 tbsp brown soft sugar
   or honey
3 tbsp gochujang chilli paste
2 tbsp soy sauce
2 garlic cloves, grated
10g root ginger, grated
1 tbsp rice wine vinegar
1 tbsp tomato ketchup

To serve
2 tsp sesame seeds
3–4 spring onions, finely
   sliced on the diagonal
Korean cucumber salad
   (see p.262)
Korean lettuce salad
   (see p.263)

Add all the sauce ingredients to a pan with 4 tablespoons of water, season with salt and pepper and heat for 4–5 minutes until combined into a glossy sauce. Keep the sauce warm until ready to serve or set it aside and reheat when needed.

Mix the ginger and cornflour in a large bowl and season with salt and pepper. Add the chicken wings and toss them until well coated, then set them aside.

Fill a large, deep pan two-thirds full with the oil and place over a medium-high heat until the oil has reached 175°C. Fry a batch of 4 or 5 wings for about 8–10 minutes until crisp and golden, turning them halfway through. Transfer them to a tray lined with kitchen paper and keep them warm in a low oven while you cook the rest. Allow the oil to come back up to temperature each time before cooking the next batch.

Once all the chicken is cooked through, pour over the hot sauce to coat all the wings well. Sprinkle with sesame seeds and spring onions and serve immediately with the salads while still crispy.

TIP
Alternatively, after coating the wings, brush them with vegetable oil and cook them in an air fryer for 10–12 minutes at 200°C until crisp and golden brown, then finish as above. You might need to cook them in batches so as not to overcrowd the fryer.

Although this is one of the most popular curries in the country, I feel it is rather ruined because it normally comes as pieces of chicken breast swimming in a not very interesting and very sweet curry sauce. I remember eating a particularly wonderful chicken korma in Lucknow in India prepared by a great cook called Rocky Mohan and this is based on his recipe. What I liked most about it was the fact that it was mild, relatively dry and delightfully grainy with ground almonds and white poppy seeds. Also, some of the spices were left whole in the finished dish – in this case, I've left in some cinnamon stick. The most important element of Rocky's dish is the marinating of the chicken in garlic and ginger and this is a much-simplified version. For me, the important thing is the choice of garam masala which I have used in place of a number of individual spices. You'll find my recipe on page 271, but I think the garam masala from an Indian company called Natco is fabulous, and their spices are in many supermarkets. I'm fond of the versions from Sainsbury's and M&S too.

CHICKEN KORMA SERVES 4

20g root ginger,
    roughly chopped
3 large garlic cloves,
    roughly chopped
2 green chillies,
    roughly chopped
400g boneless, skinless chicken
    thighs, each thigh cut in half
1½ tbsp garam masala
    (see p.271 or shop-bought)
1 tsp ground turmeric
125ml natural yoghurt
2 medium onions,
    roughly chopped
50g ghee or vegetable oil
3cm cinnamon stick
1 tsp salt
200ml coconut milk
40g ground almonds
1 tsp sugar

In a spice grinder or mini processor, blitz the ginger, garlic and green chillies to a paste. Put the chicken pieces in a bowl and combine with the paste, garam masala, turmeric and yoghurt. Cover and refrigerate for 2 hours.

Blitz the onions to a paste in a food processor, adding a splash of water if necessary. Heat the ghee or vegetable oil in a sturdy, deep-sided frying pan over a medium heat. Add the cinnamon stick and fry for 30 seconds. Stir in the onion paste and salt and fry for 10 minutes until any liquid has evaporated and the onions are softened and translucent, but not coloured.

Add the marinated chicken and any marinade to the pan and fry for a couple of minutes. Add the coconut milk, ground almonds, sugar and 100ml of water. Simmer, uncovered, for 10–15 minutes until the chicken is cooked through and the sauce has thickened a little. Add a little more water if required. Good with rice or naan bread.

I think chicken pie, and particularly chicken, ham and leek pie, is almost as popular as fish pie, or indeed shepherd's or cottage pie, with those who love British classic cooking. It's just one of those dishes that your friends don't need to ooh and ahh about, but you know they will be quietly delighted. I tend to use chicken thighs for this dish, but it's really quite nice made with leftover roast chicken or indeed turkey.

CHICKEN, HAM & LEEK PUFF PASTRY PIE SERVES 6–8

2 tbsp olive oil
About 900g skinless, boneless chicken thigh meat (about 8 thighs), cubed
20g butter
3 leeks, halved lengthways, chopped and washed well
2 celery stalks, finely sliced
50g plain flour, plus extra for dusting
100ml white wine
500ml chicken stock
150ml double cream
110g shredded ham hock
1 tsp Dijon mustard
Handful of parsley, chopped
4 thyme or tarragon sprigs, leaves stripped from stalks
500g block of puff pastry
1 egg, beaten
Salt and black pepper

You will need a pie dish measuring about 20 x 30cm.

Heat the oil in a wide frying pan and fry the chicken over a medium heat for about 6–7 minutes, stirring to cook it on all sides. Remove from the pan and set aside.

Melt the butter in the pan, add the leeks and celery and fry gently for 7–8 minutes until softened. Don't allow them to brown. Add the flour to the pan and cook for a minute, while stirring, then add the white wine and allow it to bubble up. Add the stock and cream and stir while the mixture comes to the boil and thickens. Add the chicken to the pan along with the ham and the mustard and stir to combine. Stir in the herbs and season with salt and pepper. Tip everything into your pie dish and allow to cool a little.

Preheat the oven to 200°C/Fan 180°C. On a lightly floured work surface, roll out the pastry to a thickness of 6–8mm. Brush a little beaten egg around the edge of the pie dish and lay the pastry over the filling. Using a sharp knife, trim off the excess and cut a couple of slits in the top to allow steam to escape during cooking. Brush the top with beaten egg, taking care not to glue up the vents.

Bake the pie for 25–30 minutes until golden. Serve with potatoes and steamed green vegetables.

TIP
If making with this with leftover cooked chicken or turkey, start by frying the leeks and celery in butter. Add the cold leftovers at the same time as the ham.

I'm a convert to brining chicken when I have time, as I do think it improves the flavour. Although I have some nostalgic feelings about stuffing a bird, I find it's actually much easier to cook the stuffing to perfection if done separately and these little stuffing balls do look very attractive.

ROAST CHICKEN WITH PORK, APRICOT, SAGE & PISTACHIO STUFFING BALLS SERVES 4–6

Salt
Sugar
1 x 1.7–2kg chicken
2 tbsp oil
2 large carrots, each cut
    into 3 large chunks
1 large onion, cut into wedges

Stuffing
1 tbsp oil
1 small onion, finely chopped
400g sausage meat
2 rashers of smoked streaky
    bacon, finely chopped
50g dried apricots,
    finely chopped
30g pistachio nuts, chopped
4–5 sage leaves, finely chopped
Salt and black pepper

Gravy
1 tsp plain flour
60ml white wine
500ml chicken stock

At least 8 hours or the day before you want to cook your chicken, make the brine. Pour enough water to cover your chicken into a large stockpot – maybe 3–4 litres. Add 50g of salt and 15g of sugar per litre. Heat to dissolve the sugar and salt, then take the pan off the heat and leave the brine to cool completely. Once the brine is cold, submerge the chicken in the brine, cover with a lid or foil and refrigerate for 8–12 hours.

To make the stuffing balls, heat the oil in a pan and slowly fry the onion until soft but not coloured, then leave to cool. Add the other ingredients and mix well to combine, then shape into 8–12 balls. Place in a lightly oiled tin, cover and refrigerate until ready to cook.

Preheat the oven to 230°C/Fan 210°C. Remove the chicken from the brine, drain well and discard the brine. Rub the skin with a little oil and grind over some black pepper. Put the carrots and onion in a roasting tin, drizzle with oil, then place the bird on top. Roast for 20 minutes, then turn the oven down to 170°C/Fan 150°C and cook for a further 50 minutes. Add the stuffing balls after 35 minutes.

After 50 minutes, test the chicken with a probe in the thickest part of the thigh – the temperature should be at least 67°C but ideally not more than 70°C. When the chicken is done, transfer it with the carrots and onion to a warmed carving dish. Cover and leave to rest in a warm place. If the stuffing balls need more colour, turn the oven up again and leave them for another 5 minutes.

While the chicken is resting, make the gravy. Put the roasting tin on the hob, add a teaspoon of flour to the tin and stir it into the tasty chicken juices with a wooden spoon. Add the wine and stock and bring to the boil, stirring until you have the right consistency. Season with salt and pepper and strain into a warmed gravy boat. Serve the chicken with the stuffing balls and carrots and onion.
Recipe photographs overleaf.

For the first year of The Seafood Restaurant we had to stay open during the winter, due to economic pressures, but most of the time we had no customers, apart from maybe half a dozen on a Saturday night. It was quite depressing, but we had no choice and though I wanted to put on a complete seafood menu I knew that our only customers would be locals and many of them did not care for fish that much. I recall asking Cornish comedian Jethro, one of my Wadebridge Camels rugby-playing chums, why he didn't come to my restaurant. 'I don't like fish,' he replied. I told him that we did steaks, but he said, 'They'll still taste of fish'. So, I added a few dishes such as chicken chasseur and pork chops in cider sauce to the menu. For the chicken, I used a recipe from my college textbook, *Practical Cookery*, and this is it with some changes. I cooked it over many nights, hoping there would be some customers.

CHICKEN CHASSEUR SERVES 4–6

1 x 1.5–1.7kg chicken, jointed
    into 8 pieces, or 2 bone-in
    breasts and 4 thighs
2 tbsp plain flour
25g butter
2 tbsp olive oil
180g shallots, peeled
    and quartered
2 garlic cloves, chopped
200g chestnut mushrooms,
    thickly sliced
150ml dry white wine
300ml chicken stock
2 tbsp tomato purée
Handful of parsley, chopped
A few tarragon sprigs,
    leaves roughly chopped
Salt and black pepper

Fried croutons
20g butter
1–2 tbsp oil
4–6 slices of bread, cut into
    rounds or hearts with
    a pastry cutter

Season the chicken pieces with salt and pepper and dust them liberally with flour. Melt the butter in a large frying or sauté pan, add the oil and when it's hot, fry the chicken pieces until golden brown all over. You may need to do this in a couple of batches, then put all the chicken back in the pan.

Add the shallots and garlic and cook until softened, then add the mushrooms. Fry for a couple of minutes, then add the white wine, stock and tomato purée and bring to the boil. Turn the heat down to a simmer, cover and cook over a medium heat for about 10 minutes. Remove the lid and cook for a further 10–12 minutes or until the chicken is cooked through and the sauce is slightly thickened and silky. If it looks oily, spoon off any excess oil and discard. Check the seasoning and add salt and pepper to taste.

While the chicken is cooking, prepare the croutons. Heat the butter and oil in a frying pan until foaming. Add the bread shapes and fry them on both sides until crisp and golden. Keep them warm.

Serve the chicken with the mushroom sauce spooned over and top with a crouton. Sprinkle with chopped herbs and serve with mashed potatoes or rice.

By far the most popular Thai curries in the UK are Thai green and Thai red curries. Both are made with pastes, one with red chillies, the other with green chillies and coriander. I love a Thai red chilli made with duck and something acidic like pineapple. The flavours are salty from the shrimp paste, sweet from brown sugar and coconut milk, sour from lime juice and pineapple, and hot from bird's eye chillies. I also add Kashmiri chilli powder, which gives the curry a lovely deep rich redness. This is one of those dishes where the flavour of a home-made curry paste will really shine through, but it's still worth making with a good supermarket paste.

THAI RED DUCK & PINEAPPLE CURRY SERVES 4

2 thick slices of fresh
    pineapple or 200g tinned
    pineapple, drained
1 tbsp vegetable oil
2 duck breasts
1 red onion, sliced
3–4 tbsp Thai red curry
    paste (see below or
    use shop-bought paste)
400ml tin of coconut milk
1 red pepper,
    deseeded and sliced
1 heaped tbsp sugar
1 tbsp fish sauce
Juice of ½ lime
1 red chilli, thinly sliced
    (optional)
Fresh coriander,
    roughly chopped
Salt

Red Thai curry paste
3 kaffir lime leaves,
    fresh or freeze-dried
100g shallots, roughly chopped
2 garlic cloves, peeled
1 tsp Thai shrimp paste
1 bird's eye chilli
1 tbsp Kashmiri chilli powder
½ tsp salt
½ tsp white peppercorns
½ tsp cumin seeds, toasted
1½ tsp coriander seeds,
    toasted
15g root ginger, chopped
2 lemongrass stalks,
    roughly chopped

For the curry paste, put all the ingredients in a blender or food processor and blitz.

If using fresh pineapple, peel the slices and cut them into pieces of about 1 x 3cm. If using tinned, simply drain.

Heat a wok or frying pan over a medium-high heat and add the oil. When it's hot, add the duck breasts, skin side down, and cook for 5–6 minutes. Turn them over and cook for a further 4–5 minutes, depending on their thickness. Remove them from the pan and set aside to rest for 5 minutes. Cut the breasts on the diagonal into slices about 4–5mm thick.

Drain half the fat from the pan and fry the onion until softened in the remaining fat. Add the curry paste and fry for about 2 minutes until fragrant, then add the coconut milk, red pepper, pineapple, sugar, fish sauce and slices of duck. Stir to combine and cook for a couple of minutes. Add the lime juice and season with half a teaspoon of salt. Add slices of red chilli if you like a really hot red curry and finish with the chopped coriander. Serve with plain steamed rice. *Recipe photographs overleaf.*

Crispy duck pancakes have been one of the nation's favourites for so many years, but it's always been tricky to serve them at home because those wafer-thin pancakes are astonishingly difficult to make. Now, though, Gressingham, who are by far the largest duck producers in the country, also make the pancakes and you can buy them in supermarkets. This is such a simple dish, but what genius thought to put together duck, Chinese five-spice, salt and sugar with pancakes, cucumber, spring onions and hoisin sauce? Some things are just alchemy. I'm using duck legs for my version because they're readily available and not too expensive.

CHINESE CRISPY DUCK PANCAKES SERVES 4

4 duck legs
2 heaped tsp Chinese
  five-spice powder
2 tsp brown soft sugar
1 tsp fine salt

To serve
1–2 packs of Chinese-style
  pancakes
½ cucumber, sliced into
  matchsticks about
  6cm long
4 or 5 spring onions,
  halved lengthways
  and then shredded
  into 6cm lengths
Hoisin sauce

Prick the skin on the duck legs with a cocktail stick or a fork. Mix the five-spice, sugar and salt in a small bowl, then massage it into the duck skin. For extra crispy skin, do this 24 hours ahead of time and leave the legs in the fridge, loosely covered with foil.

Preheat the oven to 180°C/Fan 160°C. Put the duck legs on a wire rack set over a roasting tin and roast them for about 1 hour and 20–30 minutes until tender on the inside and golden and crisp on the outside. Transfer to a warm plate, loosely cover with foil and leave to rest for about 10 minutes.

Shred the duck with a couple of forks, removing and discarding the bones. Warm the pancakes according to the packet instructions and serve with the duck meat, cucumber and spring onions. Have plenty of hoisin sauce available for everyone to spoon over the duck before rolling up the pancakes.

LAMB, PORK
& BEEF

Making a TV series like *Food Stories* is genuinely a journey of discovery. One of the things I found was that all the meat producers I met had animal welfare at the heart of what they did. A highlight of the series was a visit to Helen and James Rebanks at their farm in the Lake District, where they rear Herdwick sheep. I was very taken with these rugged, fell-loving animals which spend a large part of their time on common upland pastures and have really thick coats to cope with the fact they are out in all weathers. The Rebankses explained their very sound reasons for non-intensive farming based on a concern about pesticides, herbicides and fertilisers. Instead, they use their knowledge of the natural cycle of the seasons, the terrain and indeed the characteristics of the animals being reared, which makes so much sense. It is inevitable that producing what might be called ethical meat will make it more expensive, but it definitely has a much better flavour. I'm thinking here particularly of the Welsh saltmarsh lamb I cooked after visiting farmer Dan Pritchard, whose animals are left to run free on the marshes of the Gower Peninsula. Sometimes it's so hard to come to terms with the paradoxes of life, but I do like to eat some meat and that feels OK if the animals are treated well. Looking through this chapter, I find myself craving some of the dishes – steak and Guinness pie, roast beef, osso buco, rack of lamb, pulled pork – I could go on.

I made this dish for the *Food Stories* series with my son Jack and pointed out that it was my mother's recipe, all but the garlic. Maybe it's because a lot of people are needing to economise on what they cook and eat, but what the French call *réchauffés*, reheated dishes, have become very popular again. We put this on the menu at our St Petroc's Bistro recently and it sold out at every service. The only modification I've made was that my mother minced the meat with a bench-mounted mincer called a Spong, whereas I prefer to hand-chop it, which I find gives the pie filling a really interesting texture.

LEFTOVER LAMB SHEPHERD'S PIE SERVES 6

2 tbsp oil
1 large onion, chopped
3 large carrots, diced
2 garlic cloves, chopped
100ml red wine
2 tbsp tomato paste
150ml lamb, chicken or beef stock or leftover gravy
1 tbsp Worcestershire sauce
1 tsp redcurrant jelly
Small rosemary sprig
500g leftover lamb, chopped or shredded (if slow roasted)
150g fresh or frozen peas
Small handful of parsley, chopped
1kg potatoes, such as Maris Pipers, peeled and diced
50g butter
60ml double cream
Salt and black pepper

Heat the oil in a shallow flameproof casserole dish or a saucepan over a medium heat. Add the onion, carrots and garlic and fry for about 5–6 minutes until softened.

Add the red wine and tomato paste, then bring to the boil. Turn the heat down to a simmer and add the stock or gravy, Worcestershire sauce, redcurrant jelly and rosemary. Add the lamb meat, peas and parsley and season with salt and pepper. Leave to simmer gently while you prepare the potatoes.

Preheat the oven to 200°C/Fan 180°C. Boil the potatoes in a pan of well-salted water (1 teaspoon of salt per 600ml) for 10–12 minutes until tender, then drain. Heat the butter and cream in the pan. Put the potatoes through a ricer into the pan and combine, or add them to the pan, then mash. Season with salt and pepper.

If you're not using a casserole dish, transfer the lamb mixture to an ovenproof pie dish. Top the lamb with the mashed potato and fluff it up with a fork. Place in the oven and cook for about 25 minutes until golden and bubbling, then serve with leafy greens or green beans.

I remember being filmed as I cooked this dish and saying it was almost the French equivalent of our Sunday roast, but easier and quicker to cook. I've had many different accompaniments to a roast rack of lamb but for me, it's always got to be dauphinoise potatoes and I also particularly like a melange of flageolet beans, broad beans and peas, as I've suggested here. I do think, by the way, that with a rack of lamb, the tenderest part of the meat should always be served pink. Your butcher will French trim the lamb for you.

RACK OF LAMB WITH SUMMER VEGETABLE MELANGE SERVES 4

2 x 8-bone racks of lamb,
    French-trimmed
2 tbsp oil
100ml red wine or port
1 tsp redcurrant jelly
200ml lamb or beef stock
Knob of butter
Salt and black pepper

Summer vegetable melange
200g frozen broad beans,
    defrosted
15g butter
1 banana shallot, finely chopped
400g tin of flageolet beans,
    drained and rinsed
100g frozen peas, defrosted
Small handful of fresh mint
    leaves, finely chopped
Small handful of parsley,
    finely chopped
Salt and black pepper

To serve
Quick dauphinoise potatoes
    (see p.260)

Preheat the oven to 200°C/Fan 180°C. Season the lamb all over with salt and pepper. Heat the oil in a roasting tin and brown the lamb all over, then place in the oven and cook for 12–15 minutes for pink lamb or 20 minutes for medium lamb.

Cover the lamb with foil and leave to rest for 5 minutes before carving the racks into individual cutlets.

For the vegetable melange, remove the greyish outer skins from the broad beans. Bring a pan of salted water to the boil and blanch the beans, then drain and set aside.

Heat the butter in a pan over a medium heat and gently fry the shallot until soft. Add the flageolets, broad beans and peas and cook for a few minutes until the vegetables are softened but still have some bite and texture. Season with salt and pepper and stir through the herbs.

Place the roasting tin on the hob, add the wine or port and bring to the boil. Add the redcurrant jelly and stock, then season with salt and pepper. Bring to the boil and stir while the sauce reduces a little, then swirl in the butter. Add any juices from carving and serve with the lamb, dauphinoise potatoes and green vegetables.

When I visited the Rebankses at their farm in the Lake District (see page 165), Helen cooked this hotpot using the well-flavoured meat from their Herdwick sheep. She has kindly allowed me to include the recipe in this book. I was really impressed by both of them and realised how important they are as a team. You can of course make this hotpot with lamb if you can't get mutton.

HERDWICK MUTTON HOTPOT

SERVES 6

2 tbsp plain flour
1kg mutton (at room
    temperature), diced
25g lard or a splash of olive oil
2 medium onions, sliced
1 small swede or turnip,
    cut into chunks
3 carrots, cut into chunks
1 leek, cut into slices
1 parsnip, cut into chunks
50g black pudding, diced
    (optional)
570ml good-quality beef
    or chicken stock
2 tbsp tomato purée
2 tsp Worcestershire sauce
1 tbsp redcurrant jelly
    (optional)
Sprigs of rosemary or thyme
    or a bouquet garni
1 tbsp cornflour (optional)
1kg potatoes
50g butter, melted
Salt and black pepper

Preheat the oven to 180°C/Fan 160°C. Season the flour with salt and pepper, then toss the meat in the flour.

Heat the lard or olive oil in a heavy flameproof casserole dish and brown the meat. Do this in a couple of batches so you don't overcrowd the pan. Remove each batch from the pan and set it aside.

Add the onion and other vegetables to the pan and fry gently until softened. Put the meat back in the pan with the vegetables and add the black pudding, if using. Pour in the hot stock, then stir in the tomato purée, Worcestershire sauce and redcurrant jelly and tuck in the herbs. Cover the casserole dish with a lid and place it in the oven for 2 hours.

Remove the dish from the oven, stir the hotpot and check that the gravy is as thick as you want it. If necessary, mix the cornflour to a paste with a little water and add it to the hotpot to thicken the gravy.

Peel the potatoes and cut them into slices about 4mm thick. Arrange them on top of the meat and vegetables, overlapping them slightly, then brush with the melted butter. Put the lid back on the dish and put it back in the oven for another half an hour. Then remove the lid and cook for another 20–30 minutes to brown the potatoes.

In terms of the UK's favourite dishes, rogan josh is right up there with chicken tikka masala, korma and biryani. 'Rogan' means red in Hindi and 'josh' means passion. I like to think of this as a fiery red lamb curry but actually, as it's a dish originally from Persia and then Kashmir, I like to use the deep red Kashmiri chilli powder which isn't as hot as some. As you'll see in the recipe, I say to use a tablespoon of Kashmiri chilli powder but, if you can't get it, only a teaspoon of normal chilli powder. Incidentally, a Kashmiri chilli powder called deggi mirch, which is a mixture of chillies and red capsicums, is now available online or from Waitrose and would work really well in this.

LAMB ROGAN JOSH SERVES 4–6

40g ghee or vegetable oil
5cm cinnamon stick
3 dried Kashmiri chillies, torn into pieces
6 green cardamom pods, lightly bruised
4 cloves
1 large onion, chopped
3 garlic cloves, finely grated
15g root ginger, finely grated
1 tbsp Kashmiri chilli powder or 1 tsp chilli powder
2 tsp ground turmeric
2 tbsp garam masala (see p.271 or shop-bought)
1 tsp toasted ground fennel seeds, plus ¼ tsp to finish
4 tbsp tomato purée
750g boneless lamb shoulder, trimmed of excess fat, cut into 3cm cubes
1 tsp salt
175g full-fat natural yoghurt
Handful of coriander leaves, roughly chopped

To serve
Pilau rice (see p.264)
Chapatis (see p.264)

Put the oil in a large flameproof casserole dish over a medium heat. When the oil is hot, add the whole spices and fry for 1 minute, then add the onion and fry for 10 minutes until softened and golden. Stir in the garlic and ginger, fry for 1 minute, then add the ground spices (reserving the extra ground fennel) and fry for 30 seconds.

Stir in the tomato purée, then add the lamb and salt and stir to make sure the lamb is well coated with the other ingredients. Pour in 300ml of water, bring to a simmer and cover the pan. Simmer gently over a low heat for 1 hour or until the lamb is tender.

Stir in the yoghurt, then season with the extra ground fennel. Sprinkle with the coriander and serve with rice or chapatis.

You only need to walk down any high street in the UK to see how popular kebabs are. Generally, when people think of kebabs they are thinking of doner kebabs or 'elephant legs' as they are sometimes known, but in reality you are never going to be able to recreate those big cylinders of meat at home. Kofta kebabs are simply kebabs made with minced meat. As far as I am concerned, the simpler the kebab the better and the flavourings I'm using are cumin and dried mint. In Turkey, dried mint is regarded as different to fresh and is almost as important to the Turks as oregano is to the Greeks. The real pleasure of the dish is the chargrilled flavour of lamb in a nice soft flatbread.

TURKISH LAMB KOFTA KEBABS WITH YOGHURT DRESSING SERVES 8

1.2kg minced lamb
1 tbsp dried mint
2 eggs, beaten
2 garlic cloves,
   chopped or grated
1½ tsp chilli flakes
2 tsp ground cumin
Plain flour to bind,
   if necessary
Olive oil, for brushing
Salt and black pepper

Yoghurt dressing
150ml Greek yoghurt
½–1 tbsp lemon juice
4–5 fronds of dill, chopped

To serve
Flatbreads (shop-bought
   or see p.265)
Sliced red onion
Sliced tomatoes
   and/or cucumber
Shredded lettuce
Pickled chillies
Lemon wedges

Mix the kebab ingredients together in a bowl and season with a teaspoon of salt and plenty of black pepper. Add a little flour if the mixture seems too wet. Use wet hands to form the meat into sausage shapes around metal or wooden skewers – if using wooden skewers, soak them in water first. Each kebab should weigh 75–80g. Brush them with olive oil and leave them in the fridge until you're ready to cook.

Preheat a grill or a charcoal barbecue and cook the kebabs for about 8 minutes, turning them regularly. While they are cooking, stir together the ingredients for the dressing – add a splash of water if it seems too thick.

Serve with the yoghurt dressing, warm flatbreads, sliced onion, tomatoes and/or cucumber, lettuce and some pickled chillies. Offer some lemon wedges to squeeze over the kebabs.
Recipe photographs overleaf.

THE PLEASURES OF NORTHERN IRELAND AND SHORTHORN CATTLE

I had a hugely enjoyable visit to Belfast while filming *Food Stories* and then headed to the countryside to find out more about the fabulous produce of this region. On the way, I got talking to the driver about the immense economic effect of *Game of Thrones* on Northern Ireland – the perfect place for plenty of wintry landscapes coupled with comfortable hotels for the stars and crew.

Northern Ireland for me is one of the most unspoilt parts of the UK. The roads are smaller, and the farmlands and woods are bigger. We passed hedgerows cascading with May blossom, so much and so white it looked like snow, and as we arrived at the Glenarm Estate where they rear some extraordinarily fine beef, I thought that the month of May had never looked so green and grassy.

It all seemed to be part of an early summer dream to meet a herd of Shorthorns grazing the deep grass and to listen to Adrian Morrow, who has the softest, most melodious voice, explaining how incredibly calm and peaceful these cattle are – qualities that as he pointed out improve the quality of their meat. I knew about the temperament of these animals already because on the farm where I was born we kept Shorthorns – they had names like Betsy, Daisy and Violet. Some of Adrian's friendly herd came right up to me and I could smell their sweet breath. Standing there as they licked my trouser legs while I chatted with Adrian, I was once again faced with the dilemma of such wonderful creatures being turned into joints and pies. But then you say to yourself that if they weren't going to be eaten they wouldn't be there, and all you can wish for is a happy life while they are. And certainly, in the care of the charming Adrian and later with their butcher Peter Hannan, there did seem to some sense of order and harmony to their lives.

I then went to visit Hannan Meats, who do the butchering and ageing of the award-winning meat from Adrian's herd and Peter Hannan pointed out the good coating of fat on the meat from these cattle. Fat is so important for flavour and Peter says it's a sign of a happy animal, adding, 'They don't get fat unless they're happy'. I found this very comforting, having had the animals nuzzling my shins hours earlier. Peter, a man who has succeeded in his quest to produce the most excellent beef, took me through the ageing process, something he and only a few others have perfected, and which extracts the meat's moisture and concentrates its flavour. The beef is matured for 28–45 days, finishing in a chamber with a wall made with a

'Fat is so important for flavour and Peter Hannan says it's a sign of a happy animal.'

thousand blocks of Himalayan rock salt. These keep the atmosphere at a perfect degree of dryness to encourage friendly bacteria as well as preventing mould and what Peter called 'gaminess'. I remember noticing with considerable pleasure Peter's ability to tell a story. What is it about the Irish? Is it the lovely soft accent or the incredibly adroit choice of words? He could read numbers out of the telephone book, and you'd be rapt.

The last phase of my visit involved cooking two double sirloins, one barbecued over charcoal and the other just cooked in a heavy metal pan, to determine which method of cooking brought out the best in the beef, and even more importantly, the fat. We all agreed – that's me and the crew who were very enthusiastic participants – that the barbecue, while imbuing the meat with a pleasant taste of smoke, actually detracted from its extraordinary flavour. With meat this good, I say keep it simple.

I have purposely specified Cox's apples in the recipe for these, though I say it myself, fabulous sausage rolls. This is partly because they grate very easily as they are relatively firm in consistency, but also because Cox's seem to me to be more difficult to find in the autumn, compared to Pink Lady, Gala or New Zealand Braeburns, which I think is a shame. I want to encourage everyone to use Cox's. If anyone with a café fancies making these sausage rolls I'd be chuffed to bits.

PORK, COX'S APPLE & FENNEL SAUSAGE ROLLS MAKES 6–8 ROLLS

1 tbsp olive oil
1 onion, finely chopped
400g top-quality sausage meat or sausages (skins removed)
1 large or 2 small (225g) Cox's apples (or similar), peeled, cored and grated
1 tsp fennel seeds, crushed
Plain flour, for dusting
500g puff pastry
1 egg, beaten
1 tsp sesame seeds or poppy seeds (optional)
Salt and black pepper

Heat the oil in a pan and gently fry the onion over a low heat until softened but not browned. Set aside and allow to cool.

Put the sausage meat in a bowl and add the cooled fried onion, grated apple and fennel seeds, then season with salt and pepper. Set aside.

Preheat the oven to 210°C/Fan 190°C and line a baking sheet with baking parchment.

Dust your work surface with flour and roll out the pastry to about 30 x 35cm. Cut it in half lengthways so that it's a little longer than it is wide. Divide the sausage meat in half and form into 2 sausage shapes, then place 1 of these along the length of a piece of pastry. Paint one of the long edges of pastry with egg, fold the pastry over the sausage meat and press the edges together to seal. Repeat with the remaining pastry and sausage meat. Cut each roll into 3 or 4 pieces, depending on how big you want your sausage rolls.

Transfer the rolls to the lined baking sheet, brush with beaten egg and sprinkle with sesame or poppy seeds, if using. Bake for 25–30 minutes until golden and cooked through.

Prior to going to Belfast to film an episode of my latest TV series, I had almost no knowledge of Filipino cuisine. I can only say – what have I been missing? We visited an amazing stall called Kubo, run by chef Nallaine, and we filmed a traditional Filipino lunch called a 'kamayan' in which seven or eight dishes are laid out along a strip of banana leaf for everyone to help themselves and eat with their hands. The star turn for me, and the centre of the whole spread, was the pork belly adobo. Like many Filipino savoury dishes, it is cooked with dark sugar, vinegar and soy sauce which are then reduced right down to coat the meat. The adobo, which can be made with chicken instead of pork, is a typically Asian way of producing wonderfully flavoured food, while the vinegary sauce also helps to preserve the meat in a tropical climate and is utterly delicious. The mango pickle and the special rice flavoured with pandan leaf are great accompaniments. Sugar cane vinegar is much used in Filipino cooking and can be bought in the UK but if you don't have any, use apple cider vinegar.

FILIPINO PORK BELLY ADOBO WITH MANGO ATCHARA SERVES 4

2 tbsp vegetable oil
900g pork belly, skinned
   weight, cut into cubes
1 onion, sliced
9 garlic cloves, finely chopped
4 dried bay leaves
1 tbsp black pepper
250ml sugar cane vinegar
   or apple cider vinegar
125ml dark soy sauce
3 tbsp fish sauce
4 tbsp dark brown soft sugar
½ tsp salt (add at the end
   after tasting, if required)

Mango atchara
2 unripe (green) mangoes
2 tbsp raisins
250ml sugar cane vinegar
   or apple cider vinegar
45g caster sugar
1 bay leaf
2 whole cloves
2 whole garlic cloves,
   crushed or grated
3–4 peppercorns, crushed
½ tsp salt

To serve
Jasmine rice (see p.263)

Ideally, make the mango atchara a couple of hours ahead of time, but don't prepare it days ahead as the vinegar will break down the mango flesh and make it soggy.

Slice the mangoes into sticks 1–2cm thick and put them in a bowl with the raisins. Put the vinegar, sugar, bay leaf, cloves, garlic, peppercorns and salt in a pan and stir to combine. Place over a medium heat and stir until the sugar is fully dissolved. Leave to cool until the liquid is warm to the touch of your hand but not fully cooled, then pour over the mangoes and raisins in the bowl. Cover with foil.

For the pork, heat the oil in a wide pan over a medium heat. Add the pork belly and fry for about 5 minutes until browned on all sides. Then add the onion, garlic, bay leaves and black pepper and fry until the onion is translucent.

Add the vinegar, dark soy sauce, fish sauce and sugar, then stir to combine. Simmer over a medium-low heat, uncovered, for about 45 minutes until the pork is tender and the liquid has reduced to below the level of the pork. Turn the heat down low and continue to cook, stirring so the pork doesn't stick to the pan, until the liquid has thickened and is coating the pieces of pork. The soy sauce makes this quite salty already, but taste and add more salt if required.

Serve the pork with the mango atchara and jasmine rice.
Recipe photographs overleaf.

I can't imagine anyone not loving the pillowy texture of these bao buns, particularly when filled with minced pork, garlic, ginger, soy and spring onions. I have to admit that sealing the buns is bit of a faff but have a look on YouTube and see if you can master the art. Otherwise, buy ready-made buns to stuff with the filling, or just simply do your best, then turn them over and steam upside down.

STEAMED CHINESE PORK BAO BUNS MAKES 20

Bao bun dough
525g plain flour,
    plus extra for dusting
½ tsp salt
 7g sachet of fast-action yeast
25g caster sugar
1 tbsp baking powder
250ml lukewarm water
1–2 tbsp vegetable or
    sunflower oil

Filling
2 tbsp vegetable oil
1 medium onion,
    finely chopped
15g root ginger, grated
2 garlic cloves, grated
500g minced pork
1 tsp toasted sesame oil
2 tbsp Shaoxing wine
    or dry sherry
1½ tbsp soy sauce
3 tbsp oyster sauce
1 tsp brown soft sugar
Large pinch of ground
    white pepper
3–4 spring onions,
    finely sliced
1 tbsp cornflour
    mixed to a paste
    with 2 tsp water

For the dough, put all the dry ingredients in a food mixer bowl and add 200ml of the warm water. Use the dough hook to bring everything together, adding as much of the remaining 50ml of water as you need to make a soft, elastic dough. Knead in the machine for 4–5 minutes, then bring the dough together into a ball and dust with flour. (Alternatively, you can do all this by hand.) Oil a large bowl, put the ball of dough in it and cover with a clean tea towel. Leave in a warm place for 1–1½ hours until doubled in size.

For the filling, heat the oil and fry the onion, ginger and garlic until fragrant, then add the minced pork and cook for 3–4 minutes until it's a pale golden colour. Add the sesame oil, wine or sherry, soy sauce, oyster sauce, sugar, white pepper and 50ml of water and allow it to bubble up. Cook for a couple of minutes, then stir in the spring onions and the cornflour paste and continue to cook for a further minute or so until the mixture is fairly thick. Allow to cool.

When the dough is risen, divide it into 20 pieces. Roll each one into a ball, then into a disc 10–12cm in diameter and 3–4mm thick. This is best done with a small rolling pin, working outwards round the edges, turning the dough as you roll and keeping the centre slightly thicker.

Hold the disc in your non-dominant hand and add about a tablespoon of the mixture to the centre. With a clean, dry hand, start to pull up the dough over the filling, pleating the dough and crimping it a little like a pasty to close and seal the top. If the buns look messy, just ensure they are well sealed, then turn them over so that the seam is on the bottom and you have a round plain top. Place each bun on a square of baking parchment, cover with a damp tea towel and leave them to prove in a warm place for about 15 minutes.

Place a few buns in your steamer, leaving room around each one – you'll probably have to cook them in batches. Bring the water in the steamer pan up to the boil and then top with a lid. Steam for 10–12 minutes until the buns are puffed up and cooked. Turn off the heat, leave the lid on the pan and leave to rest for 5 minutes before eating.

Sweet and sour pork is still one of the most popular Chinese dishes in the UK, but I have always been a bit wary of ordering it because I've found that more often than not there's too much sweet and not enough sour. It's one of those dishes whose success depends on perfect balance, which I think this recipe has. Just to cover myself, though, I've added a touch of chilli in the form of half a teaspoon of cayenne pepper just to give the dish a little grunt, but if you're cooking it for kids who can't stand chilli, please do leave it out. Incidentally, don't let this hang around or the crisp batter, another very important feature, will get soggy.

SWEET & SOUR PORK SERVES 4

400g pork shoulder, not too
    lean, cut into 3cm chunks
1 tbsp soy sauce
1 tsp garlic powder
Large pinch of ground
    white pepper
2 tbsp cornflour
1 litre sunflower or
    vegetable oil, for frying

Sauce
2 tbsp sunflower oil
1 onion, coarsely diced
1 garlic clove, grated
20g root ginger, grated
1 red and 1 green pepper,
    deseeded and diced
4 tbsp ketchup
3 tbsp malt vinegar
1 tbsp soy sauce
2 tbsp brown soft sugar
½ tsp cayenne pepper
2 tsp cornflour, mixed with
    a tbsp of the pineapple juice
300g tin of pineapple chunks
    in juice

Batter
200g self-raising flour
1½ tsp baking powder
200ml tepid water
Salt and black pepper

To serve
Egg-fried rice (see p.263)

Toss the pork in the soy sauce, garlic powder and white pepper, then set it aside for 30 minutes while you prepare the sauce and rice.

For the sauce, heat the oil in a wok or a wide non-stick pan and gently fry the onion, garlic, ginger and peppers until slightly softened. Add 100ml of water. Mix the ketchup, vinegar, soy sauce, sugar, cayenne and the cornflour and pineapple juice together. When the peppers and onion are slightly softened, add the ketchup mixture to the pan with the chunks of pineapple and juice, then stir over a medium heat for a minute or two until thickened and glossy. Set the sauce aside and keep it warm while you cook the pork.

Dredge the pork in the cornflour and toss to coat. Make the batter by mixing the self-raising flour, baking powder, half a teaspoon of salt and some black pepper in a bowl. Whisk in the tepid water, adding a little more if needed to get a smooth batter the consistency of thick cream or custard. Drop the coated pork cubes into the batter.

Pour oil into a frying pan or wok to a depth of about 5cm and heat to 180°C. Using tongs, lift pieces of pork from the batter, which should cling to the pork, and lower them into the oil. Fry for 5–7 minutes until golden, crisp and cooked through – if you have a temperature probe the internal temperature should be 70°C. Drain on kitchen paper and keep warm while you cook the next batch. Allow the oil to come back up to temperature between batches.

When all the pork is cooked, add it to the sauce. Don't do this more than a couple of minutes ahead of time or the batter will go soggy. Serve with egg-fried rice.

Perhaps the concept of pulled pork came from the USA or Mexico, but in the UK we've taken to it with great delight. Whether served in a bun with coleslaw or as a main course, pulled pork is a derivative of the hog roast. I used to love those parties where a whole pig was roasted and the meat sliced and served in a bun with apple sauce and sage stuffing. I have a possibly irritating fondness for fennel seeds in dishes like this – you may prefer sage, but I do like the exotic flavour of fennel. Interestingly, it's unusual to find pork paired with apple in Spain and Italy, but I think it's particularly important in this dish that the richness of the pork is offset by the acidity of apple sauce.

PULLED PORK WITH COLESLAW & APPLE SAUCE SERVES 6

1½ tsp salt
½ tsp ground black pepper
3 garlic cloves, grated
1–1½ tsp fennel seeds, freshly crushed
1.5kg rindless and boneless pork shoulder, cut into 3 or 4 large pieces
350ml dry cider
3½ tbsp brown soft sugar

Apple sauce
700g Bramley apples, peeled, cored and chopped into roughly 3cm cubes
100ml cider or water
2–3 tbsp sugar

Coleslaw
½ small white, green or red cabbage, cored and finely shredded (about 300g)
½ medium red onion, finely sliced
1 small fennel bulb, very finely sliced
2 carrots, grated
3–4 tbsp mustard mayonnaise (see p.267) or mix a tsp of Dijon mustard with shop-bought mayo
Salt and black pepper

To serve
Soft bread rolls, warmed

Preheat the oven to 160°C/Fan 140°C. Mix the salt, pepper, garlic and fennel seeds and rub this seasoning into the pork. Put the meat in a flameproof casserole dish (one with a tight-fitting lid) and add the cider and sugar. Bring to the boil on the hob, then cover with the lid and transfer to the preheated oven. Cook for 2½–3 hours, until the pork is very tender.

Meanwhile, make the apple sauce. Put the apples, cider or water and sugar into a pan. Cook for 15 minutes over a medium heat until the sauce is thick and pulpy. Taste and adjust the sweetness to taste, then leave to cool to room temperature.

For the coleslaw, combine the vegetables in a large bowl. Add the mustard mayonnaise and season with salt and pepper, then mix to coat the vegetables.

Remove the casserole dish from the oven and lift out the pork. Place it on a board and, using a couple of forks, shred the meat. You want the juices left in the dish to be nice and thick so they coat the pieces of pork. If the juices in the casserole dish are runny, put the casserole dish back on the hob and reduce them to a sticky sauce. Combine the shredded pork with the reduced juices.

Split the warm bread rolls and fill them with pulled pork and coleslaw, then top with apple sauce. Serve immediately, preferably with a cold beer or cider.

Alternatively, serve the pork with root veg mash (potatoes, celeriac, carrot, swede) and maybe braised red cabbage in place of coleslaw.

I'm not sure who first recommended this dish from the Dolomites, perhaps Portia or Louisa who worked on the *Rick Stein's India* book with me, but it is, I would say, better than French onion soup. It's similar in that it contains bread and cheese, but I think it's the cabbage that makes the difference. I've skied a lot in Austria and Switzerland, although I've never been to the Italian Dolomites. I'm sure that having this soup up a mountain somewhere would be a splendid treat.

VALLE D'AOSTA CABBAGE & BREAD SOUP SERVES 4–5

300g Gruyère, Emmental or Gouda cheese, grated or thinly sliced
60g Parmesan cheese, grated
1.5 litres chicken, beef or vegetable stock
500g savoy cabbage, sliced
70ml olive oil
6 rashers of smoked streaky bacon, chopped
30g butter
1 or 2 large garlic cloves, cut in half
5–6 thick slices (about 250–280g) of stale, dry sourdough or rye sourdough bread, cut into rough pieces
Salt and black pepper

Mix all the cheese together in a bowl.

Bring the stock to the boil, add the cabbage and cook for 5 minutes, then turn off the heat and set aside.

Heat a little of the oil in a large frying pan and fry the bacon pieces until golden and starting to crisp. Remove them from the pan and set aside. Add the butter, more oil and the garlic to the pan and fry the pieces of bread until golden and crisp on all sides. Put the bacon back in the pan with the bread. Preheat the oven to 200°C/Fan 180°C.

Take a large flameproof casserole dish. Put a good layer of bread and bacon in the bottom of the dish, add a layer of cabbage on top, then some cheese. Continue layering, reserving some of the cheese for the top, then season with plenty of pepper and a little salt – not too much as the cheese is salty. Ladle over the hot stock and top with the rest of the cheese.

Place over a medium heat and bring to a simmer, then put the dish in the oven and bake, uncovered, for 30–40 minutes until hot and bubbling and all the cheese has melted. Serve in warm bowls.

Just as in the seventies and eighties most of the Indian restaurants in the UK were Bangladeshi, most of the Chinese ones of the same period were Cantonese. My early experiences of Chinese food were really just of cooking from this region. And chow mein is one of the all-time favourites. So much so that rock star Warren Zevon wrote a song called 'Werewolves of London', in which he had a werewolf hero walking the streets of Soho in the rain, looking for a beef chow mein from the restaurant Lee Hoo Fook. I well remember Lee Hoo Fook and the legendary chow mein, so when we filmed in Soho I wanted to run the song, but sadly it was far too expensive.

BEEF CHOW MEIN SERVES 3–4

400g sirloin steak,
    fat removed
1 tbsp cornflour
Large pinch of ground
    white pepper
1 tbsp oyster sauce
125ml sunflower or
    vegetable oil, plus 1 tbsp
250g dried egg noodles
    (4 nests)
150g bean sprouts
3 spring onions, trimmed
    and shredded lengthways
100g mangetout
100g shiitake mushrooms,
    sliced
3 garlic cloves, chopped
15g root ginger, grated
    or finely chopped

Sauce
½ tsp sugar
1 tbsp oyster sauce
3 tbsp soy sauce
⅛ tsp ground white pepper

To serve
2 spring onions, finely sliced
    on the diagonal

Cut the sirloin steak across into thin slices. Put the slices in a bowl, sprinkle over the cornflour and white pepper, then mix well. Add 2 tablespoons of water, the oyster sauce and the tablespoon of oil.

In a separate bowl, mix the sauce ingredients with 100ml of water and set aside.

Cook the noodles according to the packet instructions and drain them well. Heat about 100ml of the oil in a pan and when it's hot, add the drained noodles and fry them until crispy. Remove and keep warm.

Add the remaining oil to the pan and stir-fry the beef over a high heat until cooked through. Add the bean sprouts, vegetables, mushrooms, garlic and ginger and continue to stir-fry for a couple of minutes, then add the sauce and allow it to bubble and thicken.

Divide the noodles between 4 bowls and pour the steak mixture over them, ready to be mixed with chopsticks by the diner. Serve topped with the sliced spring onions.

The last time Portia, my assistant, was in Italy she noticed that the ratio of pasta to sauce in many dishes there tends to be higher than we're used to in the UK, so this lasagne has more layers of pasta than I used to have – four or five rather than three – which I think makes it much more interesting. Because of this, it's essential to use fresh lasagne, not dried, and definitely not instant lasagne which I tried recently. It's not as instant as one might think and to achieve the moisture to make it soft, it sucks everything out of the sauce and makes the dish rather dry. This is the traditional ragù recipe, but lately, I've fallen in love with my pressure cooker. I've found that if I pressure cook all the ragù ingredients together for 20 minutes – no browning needed – then take off the lid and continue cooking until everything is well reduced, the results are identical and it saves so much time and effort.

LASAGNE WITH CLASSIC PORK & BEEF RAGÙ SERVES 8

350–400g fresh lasagne sheets
Freshly grated nutmeg
1 ball of mozzarella, torn

Ragù
2–3 tbsp oil
1 onion, finely chopped
2 carrots, finely chopped
2 celery stalks, finely chopped
2 garlic cloves, finely chopped
4 rashers of smoked streaky
  bacon, finely chopped
500g minced beef
500g minced pork
175ml red wine
750ml beef or chicken stock
2 tbsp tomato paste
2 x 400g tins of chopped
  tomatoes
1 bay leaf
A few rosemary sprigs
Salt and black pepper

Béchamel
70g butter
70g plain flour
1 litre whole milk
1 bay leaf
100g Parmesan, freshly grated

For the ragù, heat the oil in a large wide pan, add the onion, carrots, celery and garlic and fry gently until softened but not coloured. Add the bacon, beef and pork and continue to fry until the meat has taken on some colour. Pour in the red wine and increase the heat to bring it to the boil. Reduce the heat again and add the stock, tomato paste and tinned tomatoes. Season with salt and pepper and add the bay leaf and rosemary. Cook for about 1½ hours over a low-medium heat until you have a rich, reduced sauce.

While the ragù is cooking, make the béchamel. Melt the butter in a large pan over a medium heat, add the flour and stir to form a paste. Cook for a minute or so, then take the pan off the heat and whisk in the milk a little at a time, until you have a lump-free sauce. Add the bay leaf, put the pan back on the heat and bring to the boil, stirring constantly, then cook until you have a thick smooth sauce. Remove the bay leaf, stir in two-thirds of the grated Parmesan and season with a little salt and pepper.

Preheat the oven to 180°C/Fan 160°C. Take a deep lasagne dish (about 20 x 30cm). Put a large spoonful of ragù in the bottom, then add a layer of lasagne sheets, cut to size if needed. Top with a layer of ragù and a drizzle of béchamel, then another layer of pasta. Continue until you have used up all the ingredients, finishing with a layer of béchamel – you should end up with 4 or 5 layers of pasta. Grate over a little nutmeg, then add the torn mozzarella and the remaining grated Parmesan.

Bake the lasagne for 45–50 minutes until bubbling and golden. Remove from the oven and allow to sit for 5–10 minutes for easier cutting. Serve with a green salad.

Traditionally, this dish is made with guanciale, cured pig's cheek, which can be bought online or in some supermarkets. Otherwise, use pancetta. Also, it includes Pecorino cheese, but you can substitute Parmesan if that's what you have. This doesn't need cream; the combination of eggs and cheese is enough to create a creamy sauce that clings to the pasta.

SPAGHETTI CARBONARA SERVES 4

400g spaghetti
175g guanciale or pancetta,
    rind removed
2 tbsp extra virgin olive oil
3 garlic cloves, finely chopped
Handful of parsley,
    finely chopped
3 large eggs, beaten
50g Pecorino cheese,
    finely grated
Salt and black pepper

Bring a large pan of well-salted water (1 teaspoon of salt per 600ml) to the boil. Add the spaghetti and cook for 9 minutes until al dente.

Meanwhile, chop the guanciale or pancetta into lardons about 5mm wide. Heat a large, deep frying pan over a medium-high heat, add the olive oil and lardons and fry until lightly golden. Add the garlic and parsley and cook for a few seconds, then remove the pan from the heat and set aside.

Drain the spaghetti well, then tip it into the frying pan with the guanciale or pancetta, garlic and parsley. Add the beaten eggs and half the Pecorino cheese and toss everything together well. Season to taste with a little salt and freshly ground black pepper. The heat from the spaghetti will be enough to partly cook the eggs but still leave them creamy.

Serve in warmed bowls and sprinkle with the remaining cheese.

The Scottish-Italian families in Glasgow and their cuisine are a much-loved part of that city, and places like the Eusebi Deli (see page 194) do classics such as osso buco, which is one of my favourite dishes, so well. This recipe first appeared in my book *Coast to Coast*, and to my mind it always has to be made with veal shin. Indeed, the name means 'hole in the bone' as the marrow has to be served with it. When we filmed this dish my son Jack made risotto Milanese, the must-have accompaniment.

OSSO BUCO WITH RISOTTO MILANESE SERVES 4

1.5kg veal shin, cut into
    slices about 4cm thick
4 tbsp olive oil
25g plain flour
1 onion, chopped
1 small carrot, chopped
1 celery stalk, chopped
Leaves from 1 rosemary sprig
2 sage leaves
150ml dry white wine
2 tomatoes, skinned
    and chopped
600ml beef stock
1 pared strip of lemon zest
Salt and black pepper

Risotto Milanese
1.2 litres beef stock
Small pinch of saffron strands
50g unsalted butter
2 shallots, finely chopped
225g risotto rice, such as
    Carnaroli or Arborio
60ml dry white wine

Gremolata
1 garlic clove, peeled
A small handful of flatleaf
    parsley leaves
1 pared strip of lemon zest

Season the slices of shin with half a teaspoon of salt and set them aside for 20 minutes before starting to cook.

Heat the oil in a flameproof casserole dish. Lightly coat the veal shin with flour and pat off any excess. Fry until browned on both sides, then transfer to a plate, being careful not to disturb the marrow. Add the vegetables, rosemary leaves and sage to the pan and fry until lightly browned. Add the wine and tomatoes and cook until the wine has almost completely evaporated.

Put the meat back in the pan and add the stock, lemon zest, half a teaspoon of salt and some pepper. Bring to the boil, then immediately turn the heat down to a simmer and cover with a lid. Leave to simmer gently for about an hour or until the meat is tender.

Remove the lid and skim off the excess fat from the surface. Increase the heat slightly and continue to simmer for 30 minutes to reduce the sauce and concentrate the flavour.

Meanwhile, make the risotto. Put the beef stock in a pan and bring it to the boil. Reduce the heat, add the saffron and keep the stock hot. Melt half the butter in a pan, add the shallots and cook them gently for 3–4 minutes, until soft but not browned. Add the rice and stir for a couple of minutes until all the grains are coated in the butter, then add the wine and let it bubble down until absorbed.

Add a ladleful of the hot stock and stir over a medium heat until it has all been absorbed before adding another. Continue like this for about 20 minutes, stirring constantly, until you have added all the stock and the rice is tender and creamy but still a little al dente. Stir in the remaining butter and season to taste with salt and pepper.

For the gremolata, chop the garlic, parsley and lemon together quite finely. Serve the risotto and osso buco on warmed plates and sprinkle with the gremolata.

WHY WE LOVE ITALIAN FOOD

Born in Italy, made in Glasgow. This is what Giovanna Eusebi says about her family and their traditions. We were sitting in her restaurant, Eusebi Deli in Park Street, Glasgow, shortly after she'd cooked me a typical southern Italian dish of artichokes stuffed with breadcrumbs, herbs, mozzarella, ham and pine nuts. She explained that dishes like this are in the *cucina povera* tradition of southern Italy, which was based on ingredients people could grow themselves, as well as pasta, beans and bread, though I suspect in the real old *povera* days there wouldn't have been as much cheese and ham as in the dish she cooked. Breadcrumbs rather than Parmesan were used to finish dishes and that is still a feature of many Sicilian recipes.

Glasgow is the most ethnically diverse city in Scotland and this has shaped their wonderfully multicultural food scene. Italians have been arriving there since the 1880s and there are now said to be more than 35,000 Italian Scots.

Giovanna herself is third-generation and what impressed me was that even after such a long time in the UK, the Italian traditions in her family are still so strong. I think that's what makes the Italian presence in Glasgow so important to the cuisine of the city. It's not just about lots of pizza, spaghetti Bolognese and lasagne – it's also stuffed artichokes, osso buco and risotto Milanese. I must point out, though that there are excellent versions of spaghetti Bolognese and so on in many parts of the UK today and that is really to do with the enormous popularity of Italian food in this country. When I was thinking of what to include in this book and accompanying TV series about the nation's favourite dishes, Glasgow and the Italians, not only for main dishes but for ice cream too, came readily to mind.

So why is Italian food so popular, not just here in the UK but all over the world? Thinking of another great cuisine, why aren't there great French restaurants all over Glasgow? Perhaps part of the answer is that while Italian food originated in people's homes, French cuisine, as we knew it in England in the fifties, sixties and seventies, was largely a product of the restaurants that opened after the French Revolution, when so many cooks who had been employed by the nobility were thrown out of their jobs and then opened restaurants. What we all really love to eat is comforting home cooking, using delicious ingredients like garlic, tomatoes, olive oil, basil, Parmesan and pasta – all of which feature so largely in Italian cuisine.

'Giovanna herself is third-generation and what impressed me was that even after such a long time in the UK, the Italian traditions in her family are still so strong.'

The food Giovanna cooks is from the heart and inspired by her grandmother. She says that to cook like an Italian, you must start with respect for the ingredients. I do have to say that the Italians know how to ladle it on, and I say this with great love. For instance, Giovanna says her grandmother, Nonna Maria, would cradle flour in her hands like a holy relic, whispering 'vita' – life.

To digress for a moment and warming to the theme of why we love Italians and their cuisine so much, I once did a television programme about the links between music and food in Italy and how Italian opera composers like Verdi, Puccini and Rossini featured eating and drinking in so many of their operas. Think of such scenes as the drinking song in Verdi's *La Traviata* and the very lively restaurant scene in *La Bohème*. Indeed, Rossini later in his life became far more interested in food than opera. His fame extended beyond his own country's borders with the luxurious tournedos Rossini, a dish of steak topped with fois gras and truffle, that was named after him but created in Paris.

The idea was not ultimately something that could be proved in the programme, but so many conductors, sopranos and directors were absolutely in agreement that Italian food and opera were forever intertwined. We left Italy having seen three or four thoroughly great operas in wonderful theatres and a good time was had by all.

Returning to Glasgow, I finished my visit there by going to the University Café, where the Verrecchia family have been serving food and their own ice cream since 1918. I enjoyed a splendid knickerbocker glory, possibly an American invention originally but made with sublime Italian gelato and served with the generosity of spirit that is characteristic of this great city.

Lots of people hate offal, including liver and onions. Personally, I always want to order it, whether in its British form or the more elegant *fegato alla Veneziana*. For me, I think the revelation came after having eaten hard, thick slabs of ox or pigs' liver and onions at school. To then experience thinly sliced calves' liver, pink and meltingly soft, was a bit like discovering espresso coffee. Liver became very smart. Having said all this, I think that bacon, which is an English addition, is a very agreeable modification and makes a nice foil to the liver.

FEGATO ALLA VENEZIANA SERVES 2

15g butter
1 large onion, thinly sliced
Pinch of sugar
1½ tsp balsamic vinegar
100–150ml beef stock
6 thinly sliced rashers of
    streaky bacon, rind removed
300g calves' liver, thinly sliced
1 tbsp flour, for dusting
1 tbsp sunflower oil
Salt and black pepper

To serve
Italian-style greens (see p.258)
Mashed potato

Melt the butter in a frying pan, add the onion and sugar and fry over a medium heat for 7–8 minutes until the onion is nicely browned, stirring frequently. Season with salt and pepper, then add the balsamic vinegar and stock – the exact amount will depend on the size of your pan and how quickly the liquid cooks down – and leave it to bubble up for a few seconds. You're aiming for a nice thick consistency. Take the pan off the heat and keep the onions warm.

Heat a grill or a griddle pan to high and cook the bacon until crisp at the edges. Keep it warm.

Season the liver slices with salt and pepper and dust them with flour. Add the oil to another frying pan and cook the slices of liver over a high heat for about 30 seconds on each side. The liver should be browned on the outside and pink and juicy in the middle.

Serve the liver on warm plates with the bacon and onions, the greens and some mashed potato.

I'm inordinately fond of pot-roasting meat, particularly when it is a slightly less than tender cut, like brisket. When you open the pot towards the end of the cooking time, the aroma of onions, celery, carrots and beer is as comforting as the smell of smoke from a wood fire in an open hearth.

POT-ROAST BRISKET WITH PARSLEY DUMPLINGS SERVES 6

4 tbsp vegetable
   or sunflower oil
1.3kg boned and rolled
   beef brisket joint
20g butter
2 onions, chopped
2 celery sticks, sliced
4 carrots, each cut
   into 3 pieces
200ml beer
500ml rich beef stock
1 bay leaf
2 fresh thyme sprigs
1 tsp sugar
Chopped parsley
Salt and black pepper

Dumplings
150g self-raising flour
75g suet
Small handful of parsley,
   chopped

To serve
Colcannon (see p.262)
Horseradish & apple sauce
   (see p.267)

Preheat the oven to 160°C/Fan 140°C.

Heat the oil in a large flameproof casserole dish and brown the brisket on all sides, then remove it and set aside. Add the butter to the pan, reduce the heat and cook the onions, celery and carrots for 5–6 minutes until golden.

Add the beer, beef stock, bay leaf, thyme and sugar, then season well with salt and pepper. Bring to the boil, then immediately turn the heat down to a simmer and put the beef back in the pan. Cover with a lid, transfer to the preheated oven and cook for 2½–3 hours, turning the beef after the first hour.

Remove the beef from the pan, transfer it to a plate and cover with foil to keep it warm.

Mix the dumpling ingredients in a bowl and season with salt and pepper. Add enough water (about 100ml) to make a soft dough, then with floured hands, shape the dough into 6 balls. Bring the juices in the pan back to the boil, adding a little more stock or water if the pan looks dry. Add the dumplings, cover with the lid and return to the oven for 20 minutes until the dumplings are risen and fluffy.

Carve the beef into thick slices. Taste the juices and add more seasoning if needed. Serve the beef with the dumplings, vegetables and meat juices and sprinkle with a little parsley. Colcannon and some horseradish and apple sauce are good accompaniments.

This is a classic Tex-Mex dish which is almost as popular in the UK as in the USA. It's very easy to make and is begging to be cooked for large numbers of people. And as Portia, my very able assistant, says, it's ideal for a bonfire night party. What I love most about chilli con carne are the bits you add to it. I've specified Lancashire cheese because it's crumbly, but any hard cheese will do. There must be soured cream and coriander and I love a few wedges of ripe avocado. Chilli freezes well and it's always useful to have things that you can make in advance for parties. Many people are convinced that stews and dishes like chilli taste better when reheated. I wonder, though, if this is simply because when you've just cooked something you think it's not as good as it should be, even if everyone else says its fabulous, but the next day you come to it just like anyone else. It's not your immediate creation any longer.

CHILLI CON CARNE SERVES 8

50g dried guajillo chillies
400ml hot water
400g tin of chopped tomatoes
2 tbsp chipotles in adobo sauce
    (shop-bought or see p.268)
1 tbsp tomato paste
2 tbsp vegetable oil
2 onions, chopped
3 garlic cloves, chopped
150g chorizo, chopped
750g minced beef (not too lean)
1½ tsp ground cumin
1½ tsp oregano
500ml beef stock
1 bay leaf
1 large red pepper,
    deseeded and diced
400g tin of black beans
    or kidney beans, drained
20g dark chocolate
    (at least 70% cocoa solids)
Salt and black pepper

To serve
Fresh coriander, chopped
Lancashire cheese, crumbled
Soured cream
Avocado, peeled,
    stoned and diced
Freshly boiled long-grain
    rice or corn tortillas

Shake the seeds from the guajillo chillies. Toast the chillies in a dry frying pan until fragrant but not burnt, then soak them in the hot water for 15 minutes. Put them and the tomatoes in a blender with about half of the chilli soaking liquid (reserve the rest for later), the chipotles in adobo sauce and tomato paste and blend until smooth.

Heat the oil in a large pan over a high heat and fry the onions, garlic, chorizo and beef until the beef is browned. Add the cumin and oregano and continue to fry for a minute or so, then add the contents of the blender, the beef stock and bay leaf. Season with salt and pepper. Bring to a simmer, then put a lid on the pan, turn the heat down and continue to simmer for about an hour.

Take the lid off the pan, add the red pepper and black beans, then continue to cook for 30–40 minutes, uncovered. Add more of the chilli soaking liquid if the mixture starts to dry out. Taste and add more salt and pepper if needed, then turn off the heat. Add the dark chocolate and stir until melted.

Scatter with coriander, cheese, soured cream and avocado and serve with rice or tortillas.

In 1976, looking to make the whole building that's now The Seafood Restaurant with rooms pay, we turned the first floor into a hamburger restaurant. I'd inherited an old chargrill from the club that I bought in 1975 and I discovered a company selling American hamburger patties and jars of Bick's cubit relish. There was no extraction in the kitchen on that floor, so I took out four small panes from a large window and screwed in a wooden panel with a hole cut out for a 16-inch Vent-Axia fan. I put the grill under the window to try to keep the smoke down, but on the first really busy night, the heat from the grill melted the fan which then fell into it. From then on, the two boys cooking in the Great Western Hamburger restaurant wore masks made out of damp tea towels and goggles, as there was so much smoke. Maybe there's a lot to be said for the improvements in health and safety since then. But the burgers were wonderful. As far as I can recall, this is what we put into them and I've come up with a new relish recipe. I have written many burger recipes, but the beef patty has always been the same.

CLASSIC BURGER, WITH TOMATO & RED PEPPER RELISH SERVES 4

Burgers
500g chuck steak, coarsely
  minced with 75g beef fat
1 tsp salt
1 tsp ground black pepper
Sunflower oil, for cooking

Tomato & red pepper relish
2 tbsp vegetable oil
1 onion, finely chopped
2 garlic cloves, chopped
1 red pepper, deseeded
  and finely chopped
1 tsp yellow mustard seeds
½ tsp chilli flakes
75ml malt, cider
  or wine vinegar
75g brown soft sugar
2 tbsp tomato paste
400g tin of chopped tomatoes
Salt and black pepper

To serve
4 burger buns, sliced
  through the middle
Mustard mayonnaise
  (see p.267)
4 slices of Cheddar cheese
½ red onion, thinly sliced
1 beefsteak or large
  tomato, sliced
Handful of salad leaves
2 dill pickles, sliced

For the relish, heat the oil in a pan over a medium heat. Gently fry the onion, garlic and red pepper for a minute or so – you want them to retain their crunch. Add the mustard seeds, chilli flakes, vinegar, sugar, tomato paste and tomatoes, then season with salt and pepper. Bring to the boil and stir, then cook over a medium-high heat for about 10 minutes until the relish has thickened but the vegetables still retain some bite. Cool and store in a large jam jar in the fridge.

For the burgers, mix the meat with the salt and pepper. Divide the mixture into 4 balls, then flatten them to form burger patties.

Heat a frying pan or griddle pan until hot. Drizzle with a little sunflower oil and fry the burgers until cooked as desired – a meat probe is best for checking this. For medium, cook for 6–7 minutes on each side to an internal temperature of 55°C. For well done, cook for at least 8 minutes on each side to an internal temperature over 70°C. When the burgers are ready, set them aside while you toast the cut sides of the buns in the pan.

Assemble the burgers. Dollop some mustard mayo on the bottom bun, top with a burger, a slice of cheese, sliced onion and tomato, salad leaves and dill pickles. Serve with the relish.

This book is not only about the nation's favourite dishes but also some very popular food in sometimes quite quirky scenarios. I'm thinking of Ikea, where people are known to visit for the sole reason of having the Swedish meatballs, often queuing for them. The stores now sell packs of frozen meatballs. I like the fact that rather than coming with a standard tomato sauce, they have a cream gravy. The flavour of the meatballs with a bit of allspice and white pepper is quite special too. They are normally served with peas and boiled or mashed potatoes.

SWEDISH MEATBALLS WITH CREAM SAUCE SERVES 4

50g breadcrumbs
50ml milk
325g pork sausage meat
  (or use pork mince and
  add some beaten egg)
325g minced beef
¼ tsp ground white pepper
½ tsp ground allspice
1 tsp salt
2 tbsp vegetable
  or sunflower oil

Sauce
300ml beef stock
120ml double cream
1 tsp Dijon mustard
1 tsp redcurrant jelly
  (optional but good)
1 tsp soy sauce
1½ tsp cornflour (optional)
Salt and a pinch of
  white pepper

Put the breadcrumbs in a large bowl, add the milk and leave until it has been absorbed. Add the sausage meat (or pork mince and beaten egg), minced beef, spices and salt. Mix well and then divide into about 24 walnut-sized balls.

Heat the oil in a large frying pan, add the meatballs and fry them over a low heat for about 15 minutes until golden and cooked through. Remove them from the pan and cover with foil to keep warm.

Add the beef stock and cream to any juices in the pan, then the mustard, the redcurrant jelly, if using, and soy sauce. If the sauce needs thickening, mix the cornflour with a little water to make a thin paste and add it to the sauce. Bring to the boil, then turn down to simmer and season with salt and pepper to taste.

Put the meatballs back in the pan with the sauce or serve the meatballs with the sauce in a jug for everyone to add for themselves at the table. Mashed potatoes, peas and lingonberry or cranberry sauce are good accompaniments.

I made this pie with chuck steak bought from a wonderful butcher in Northern Ireland called Peter Hannan (see page 176). He ages his beef in a room lined with big blocks of pink Himalayan rock salt to keep the air perfectly conditioned. Even chuck in a stew or a pie like this one benefits from being aged. I quite enjoyed my thought when I was filmed eating this dish, about the pie filling being really dark and going perfectly with a pint of Guinness. Northern Ireland on a plate, I decided.

STEAK & GUINNESS PIE SERVES 4–6

1kg aged chuck steak,
    cut into 3cm cubes
20g plain flour
60g lard
2 onions, sliced
2 celery sticks, sliced
2 carrots, sliced
2 tbsp tomato purée
500ml Guinness
200ml beef stock
200g chestnut mushrooms,
    thickly sliced
1 tbsp soy sauce
1–2 tsp sugar
3 bay leaves
3 thyme sprigs
Salt and black pepper

Shortcrust pastry
200g plain flour,
    plus extra for dusting
½ tsp salt
50g very cold butter, cubed
50g very cold lard, cubed
2 tbsp very cold water
1 egg, beaten

Toss the cubed steak in the flour. Heat half the lard in a flameproof casserole dish and when it's hot, add the beef and brown it all over. You may need to do this in a couple of batches. Add the onions, celery, carrots and tomato purée and fry gently until the vegetables are soft and golden.

Add the Guinness, stock, mushrooms, soy sauce, sugar, bay leaves and thyme and season generously with salt and pepper. Bring to the boil, then turn the heat down until just simmering. Cover with a lid and cook on the hob for 1½–2 hours, until the beef is tender.

If the filling looks too runny, transfer the meat and veg with a slotted spoon to your pie dish and boil the liquid hard to reduce. Then combine with the meat and allow to cool while you make the pastry.

Sift the flour and salt into a food processor or a mixing bowl. Add the chilled butter and lard and pulse or work together with your fingertips until the mixture looks like coarse breadcrumbs. Add enough water to bring it together into a dough, then turn out on to a lightly floured surface. Shape into a disc about 4–5cm thick, then cover and chill until ready to use.

Preheat the oven to 190°C/Fan 170°C. Spoon the cooled filling into the pie dish. Add a pie funnel if you have one to lift the middle of the pastry off the filling. Roll out the pastry on a floured surface to the right size for your pie dish. Brush the edges of the dish with some beaten egg to help the pastry stick, then lay the pastry over the filling. Make a little cut in the centre to release the steam, then brush the pastry with beaten egg.

Bake in the preheated oven for 30–35 minutes until golden. Nice with boiled potatoes and green vegetables.
Recipe photographs overleaf.

After red and green curries, Massaman beef curry is probably the most popular Thai dish in the UK. It's the Thai version of the Muslim curries of northern India and made really special by the use of fish sauce and tamarind in the curry as well as shrimp paste and lemongrass in the massaman paste. But the spice that excites me is black cardamom, which gives the curry a slightly smoky flavour. Incidentally, black cardamom also makes a Christmas mulled wine quite special. I've included my recipe for the massaman paste on page 271, but you can buy it ready-made in large supermarkets.

THAI MASSAMAN BEEF CURRY SERVES 8

1.5kg chuck steak,
    cut into 5cm cubes
2 x 400ml tins of coconut milk
1 tsp salt
6 black cardamom pods,
    bruised
10cm cinnamon stick
350g waxy potatoes, diced
8 shallots, peeled and
    halved lengthways
130–150g massaman paste
    (see p.271 or shop-bought)
2 tbsp fish sauce
2 tsp tamarind paste
1 tbsp brown soft sugar
    or palm sugar

To serve
75g dry roasted peanuts,
    roughly chopped
Small handful of Thai basil
    or fresh coriander,
    roughly chopped

Take a large pan with a lid and add the beef, one tin of coconut milk and 200ml of water, plus the salt, cardamom pods and cinnamon stick. Bring to simmering point, then partially cover the pan with the lid, leaving a gap for steam to escape. Leave to cook over a low- medium heat for 2 hours until the beef is almost tender.

Uncover the pan and add the potatoes, shallots, massaman paste, fish, sauce, tamarind paste, sugar and the rest of the coconut milk. Cook gently for about 30 minutes, uncovered, until the potatoes are tender.

Serve, garnished with the roasted peanuts and Thai basil or coriander.

I have to admit to having written two recipes for beef and Yorkshire pudding in previous books, but they were both for sirloin. This recipe is for topside, which is cheaper and much more readily available, but needs to be cooked at a lower temperature after the initial high temperature period. I also wanted to highlight the importance of Yorkshire pudding, which, in this case I favour making as a single large showstopper in a roasting tin. I was lucky enough to have a conversation with Elaine Lemm when filming at the Star Inn at Harome near Castle Howard in North Yorkshire for my *Food Stories* series. Elaine quotes food historian Jennifer Stead and a famous essay of hers, 'Yorkshire pudding and parkin'. In this she says, 'The fact that they require spanking-hot fat, explosions as the batter hits it, fierce heat, and crisp results, may explain why it has often been said that only Yorkshire folk – those possessing the Yorkshire temperament – can make a true Yorkshire pudding.' Sounds a bit like the legendary Yorkshire cricketer Freddie Truman to me. In case you don't have a food temperature probe, I have given some accurate cooking times for the beef by weight, but I suggest you buy one. It'll change your life!

ROAST TOPSIDE OF BEEF WITH YORKSHIRE PUDDING SERVES 6–8

2kg topside, rolled with
   a good layer of fat
1 onion, thickly sliced
1 carrot, thickly sliced
Salt and black pepper

Gravy
1½ tsp plain flour
500ml beef stock
   or hot water

Yorkshire pudding
225g plain flour
½ tsp salt
4 eggs
300ml whole milk
150ml water

To serve (optional)
Roast potatoes (see p.261)
Cheesy leeks (see p.258)
Glazed carrots (see p.258)
Horseradish sauce
   and/or mustard

Preheat the oven to 230°C/Fan 210°C. Weigh the joint of beef. Put the onion and carrot slices into the centre of a roasting tin. Rub the beef joint with salt and pepper, then put it on top of the vegetables and place the tin on the top shelf of the oven. Roast for 30 minutes to brown the meat.

Lower the oven temperature to 160°C/Fan 140°C, then time the beef cooking from this point. Allow the following times per 500g: 10 minutes for very rare meat, 12 minutes for rare, 15 minutes for medium and 20 minutes for well done. For example, cook a 2kg joint for 40 minutes if you want very rare meat. If you do have a temperature probe, check the meat towards the end of the cooking time, using the guide on page 275.

Make the Yorkshire pudding batter. Sift the flour and salt into a bowl, make a well in the centre, then break in the eggs. Using a balloon whisk, beat the eggs and flour together well, then gradually beat in the milk and water to make a smooth batter. Make sure that it is free of lumps and has the consistency of double cream, then leave to rest for 30 minutes.

When the beef is done, remove it from the oven and transfer it to a carving board. Increase the oven temperature to 220°C/Fan 200°C. Cover the beef with foil and leave it to rest in a warm place for 30 minutes. Pour the excess fat from the roasting tin into a small bowl, leaving a teaspoon or so in the tin.

Add about 2 tablespoons of the beef fat to another roasting tin, about 20 x 30cm in size. Place it in the oven for 5–10 minutes until the fat is really hot, then pour in the pudding batter. Place in the oven immediately and cook for 25–30 minutes until well risen and golden brown. Don't open the door for at least the first 15 minutes.

To make the gravy, place the beef roasting tin directly over a medium heat on the hob and, if the onion slices are not already a rich brown, cook them for a few more minutes. Sprinkle in the flour, stir well and then add a little beef stock or water and scrape the base of the tin with a wooden spoon to release all the cooking juices. Gradually add the rest of the beef stock or water and simmer until reduced to a well-flavoured gravy. Strain into a clean pan, season and keep hot.

Uncover the beef and pour any juices into the gravy. Carve the beef into thin slices.

Serve the roast beef on warmed plates with the Yorkshire pudding, roast potatoes, cheesy leeks, glazed carrots, the hot gravy and some horseradish sauce and/or mustard. If the vegetables the beef was cooked with look acceptable, they could be served too. *Recipe photographs overleaf.*

TIP
If you prefer to make individual Yorkshires, put half a teaspoon of beef fat into each hole of a 12-hole muffin tray. Place it on the top shelf of the oven for 5 minutes until the fat is very hot. Remove and pour enough batter into each hole to fill it three-quarters full. Put the tray back in the oven and cook for 25–30 minutes until the Yorkshires are puffed up and golden. Don't open the oven door for at least the first 15 minutes.

PUDDINGS
& BAKES

When my friends taste my double-crust apple pie they are apt to say that it reminds them of their mums' pies or their grandmas'. A fruit pie like this doesn't need to be all singing and dancing but understated, allowing you to enjoy the sandiness of a good shortcrust pastry made with butter and lard. The essential accompaniment, of course, is custard. Because of childhood memories, I still like Bird's custard powder, but I do love the pots you can get in the supermarket chiller cabinets these days. May I also draw your attention to my custard recipe on page 270. I don't know if it's something about getting a tiny bit older, but these days I love afternoon tea: simply a cup of tea, Lapsang Souchong in my case, and a piece of cake. And because it's almost more about the tea, the simpler the cake the better. A Victoria sponge, or more correctly, a Victoria sandwich, is just that and the filling of the sandwich is simply jam. For me, it must be raspberry jam. I'm not supposed to mention particular makes, but specifically a French brand with a top like a red gingham tablecloth. In this chapter you will find apple pie and a few cakes, plus some blasts from the past such as baked Alaska and knickerbocker glory.

Rachel Green, whose great-grandmother's recipe this is, explained to me when we were filming at her farmhouse in Lincolnshire that plum bread doesn't actually contain any plums but instead uses currants, sultanas, raisins and mixed peel. Historically, all dried fruit was known as plums, hence the name of this bread. We ate it with some Lincolnshire poacher cheese, a perfect combination. I do note that because the dough is very rich it does take a fair time to rise. This is my version of her recipe, using fast-action dried yeast instead of fresh.

GRANNY GREEN'S LINCOLNSHIRE PLUM BREAD

MAKES 2 LOAVES

40g butter, plus extra
    for greasing
80g currants
80g sultanas
80g raisins
390g strong plain flour,
    plus extra for dusting
15g fast-action dried yeast
40g lard
1 tsp salt
1 tsp ground cinnamon
½ tsp allspice
A few rasps of nutmeg
100g brown soft sugar
150ml lukewarm milk
1 large egg, lightly beaten
40g mixed peel

To serve
Butter
Hard cheese, such as
    Lincolnshire Poacher

Grease 2 x 450g loaf tins with a little butter.

Put the currants, sultanas and raisins in a bowl and cover them completely with warm water. Leave to soak for 5 minutes, then strain the soaked fruits and leave them in a sieve over a bowl until needed.

Put the flour, yeast, butter, lard, salt, spices and sugar into a large mixing bowl. Add the milk and beaten egg and combine, mixing all the ingredients together with a dough hook or your hands to form a dough – add a little extra milk if necessary. Continue to knead the mixture for at least 10–12 minutes until the dough is soft and elastic.

Mix in the soaked dried fruit and the mixed peel and knead again until evenly distributed. Cover the bowl with a tea towel or cling film and leave it in a warm place for 1–2 hours until doubled in size.

Tip the dough out on to a lightly floured work surface and gently knock it back. Divide the mixture in half and shape into the loaf tins. Cover the tins again and leave them in warm place until almost doubled in size. Preheat the oven to 200°C/Fan 180°C.

Bake the loaves for 20 minutes. Turn the oven temperature down to 180°C/Fan 160°C and bake for a further 15–20 minutes until the loaves are nicely risen, light brown in colour and they sound hollow when tapped from underneath.

Remove the loaves from the oven and leave them to cool slightly in the tins, then remove and place on a wire rack to cool completely. Slice and serve the bread as it is or toasted, with butter and a wedge of cheese, such as Lincolnshire Poacher.

I don't know why, but I don't think of plums as a common theme in British desserts, although the acidity of the slightly under-ripe plums you generally find in the supermarket is perfect for something like a crumble. For the topping, I particularly like part of the flour being replaced with ground almonds, and a bit of demerara sugar adds a lovely deep colour.

SUPERMARKET PLUM CRUMBLE SERVES 6–8

Juice of ½ orange
1 tsp cornflour
900g plums, halved
    and stoned
50g sugar

Topping
275g plain flour
175g cold butter
100g demerara sugar
50g ground almonds

To serve
Clotted cream, custard
    or vanilla ice cream

Preheat the oven to 190°C/Fan 170°C. Mix the orange juice and cornflour and combine with the plums and sugar. Tip into an ovenproof dish.

For the topping, put the flour and butter into a food processor and pulse together a few times until the mixture looks like coarse breadcrumbs. (Alternatively, put the flour and cubed butter in a bowl and rub them together with your fingertips.) Stir in the sugar and the ground almonds, then sprinkle the mixture over the plums.

Bake for about 45 minutes until the plums are tender and the top is golden brown. Serve with clotted cream, custard or vanilla ice cream.

In 2006 Sas and I started a business in Sydney called Palm Beach Cupcakes. We rented a unit in Artarmon. The recipes were really good: lemon drizzle, which we called luv'n'lemon, butterscotch, chocolate and fresh raspberry. In the brochure I wrote that everyone loves cupcakes, as they remind us of childhood and the fun of birthday parties. Sadly, the venture didn't work, mainly now I realise, because we didn't have a shop to sell the cupcakes in and also because we couldn't afford a full-time baker. We had no sales staff to speak of and I did some deliveries myself. I recall driving to Clareville on Pittwater to deliver a box of our cakes and the English couple who were renting a house there exclaiming with some surprise, 'What's the fish cook Rick Stein doing delivering cupcakes?' I think the one missing jewel in our cupcake repertoire was red velvet.

RED VELVET CHOCOLATE & CHERRY CUPCAKES

MAKES 12 CUPCAKES

215g plain flour
15g cocoa powder
200g caster sugar
1 tsp baking powder
¼ tsp bicarbonate of soda
Pinch of salt
170g butter, melted
3 medium eggs, beaten
1 tsp vanilla extract
100ml buttermilk
30ml red food colouring

Ganache icing
180g dark chocolate, chopped
250ml double cream

Jammy cherry compote
250g stoned cherries
   (fresh or frozen), halved
50g caster sugar

To decorate
12 fresh cherries on stalks

First make the ganache. Put the chocolate in a heatproof bowl. Heat the cream in a small pan until it is steaming and just below boiling point. Pour it over the chocolate and leave to sit undisturbed for 30 seconds. Start stirring slowly, working from the middle outwards until you have a smooth ganache. If there are still a few lumps of unmelted chocolate, place the bowl over a pan of simmering water and stir until everything is melted and smooth. Allow to cool completely.

Preheat the oven to 190°C/Fan 170°C. Put 12 muffin cases into a deep muffin tin.

Sift the flour, cocoa, sugar, baking powder, bicarb and salt into a large bowl. Add the melted butter, beaten eggs, vanilla, buttermilk and food colouring, then stir well until thoroughly combined. Divide the mixture between the 12 cases and bake the cakes in the middle of the oven for 15–20 minutes or until well risen and the tops are springy.

Meanwhile, put the cherries and sugar in a pan and place over a medium-high heat. Cook until jammy, then set aside to cool.

Once the cupcakes have cooled, use an apple corer or teaspoon to scoop out some of the centre from each cake and fill the holes with cherry compote. Using a palette knife, spread some of the ganache over the top of each cake and decorate with a cherry on a stalk. *Recipe photographs overleaf.*

I can remember saying when we filmed making this Black Forest gateau that this treat rather lost its charm after it became a staple of the freezer cabinet in the seventies and eighties. You can imagine it on the dessert trolley at Fawlty Towers. Actually, the real thing is a riot of excess and a true celebration of great juicy cherries. This recipe brings back memories of filming at Little Sharsted Farm in Kent where I was far more interested in cramming the wonderfully sweet fruit, fresh from the trees, into my mouth than talking to the camera.

BLACK FOREST GATEAU WITH FRESH CHERRIES SERVES 8–10

200g butter, cubed,
    plus extra for greasing
200g dark chocolate
    (70% cocoa solids),
    broken up
100ml very hot water
175g plain flour
30g cocoa powder
1 tsp baking powder
¼ tsp bicarbonate of soda
175g caster sugar
175g brown soft sugar
3 large eggs, beaten
75ml buttermilk or
    natural yoghurt

Cherry compote
750g cherries, stoned,
    plus 8–10 whole cherries
    on stalks, to decorate
50g caster sugar

To finish
3 tbsp kirsch or cherry brandy
500ml double or
    whipping cream
50g dark chocolate
    (70% cocoa solids),
    shaved with a microplane
    or potato peeler

For the compote, put the cherries and the sugar (no water) into a pan and place over a medium-high heat. Cook until the cherries have a jammy consistency but still retain their shape.

Preheat the oven to 180°C/Fan 160°C. Grease 3 x 20cm round sandwich tins and line them with baking parchment.

Put the chocolate, butter and hot water into a bowl and set it over a pan of simmering water. Stir gently until everything has melted and combined. Remove from the heat and set aside to cool slightly.

Mix all the dry cake ingredients together in a bowl. Make a well in the centre and add the eggs and the buttermilk or yoghurt, then the chocolate mixture. Whisk with an electric hand whisk to make a lump free batter.

Divide the mixture between the 3 tins (each will only be about a third full) and bake for 20–25 minutes until cooked through and slightly shrinking from the edges of the tins. Transfer the cakes to a wire rack and leave them to cool in their tins, then turn them out and peel off the baking paper. Drizzle each cake with a tablespoon of kirsch or cherry brandy.

Whip the cream to soft peaks. Spoon about a quarter of it into a piping bag fitted with a large star nozzle and set it aside in the fridge.

Put one sponge on a plate, spread it with half of the cream, then half the cherry compote. Add another sponge on top, spread with the rest of the cream and the compote, then top with the third sponge. Pipe rosettes on top of the cake with the cream you set aside in the piping bag, and add a whole cherry to each one. Scatter over the chocolate shavings.

Sara Lee blueberry cheesecakes were a must-have sensation back in the seventies. But just as with the Black Forest gateau on page 222, familiarity inevitably bred contempt. Time passes, though, and things change, so it's lovely to revisit such a perfectly conceived combination of flavours.

BAKED VANILLA CHEESECAKE WITH BLUEBERRY TOPPING SERVES 8–10

140g butter, melted,
    plus extra for greasing
280g digestive or ginger
    nut biscuits
500g full-fat cream cheese
300g soured cream
150g golden caster sugar
3 large eggs, beaten
4 tsp vanilla extract

Blueberry topping
300g blueberries
65g caster sugar
Juice of ½ lemon
4 tsp cornflour

Grease and line the base of a 23cm springform cake tin. Put the biscuits in a plastic bag and bash with a rolling pin until they resemble breadcrumbs. Tip them into a bowl and mix with the melted butter, then transfer to the cake tin. Press and flatten the mixture with the back of a spoon, then cover and refrigerate for 30 minutes.

Preheat the oven to 160°C/Fan 140°C. Put the cream cheese, soured cream, sugar, eggs and vanilla extract into a large bowl and, using an electric hand whisk, beat until smooth. Pour the mixture on top of the chilled biscuit base.

Bake the cheesecake for 50–60 minutes until just set, then leave it to cool in the oven with the door ajar for 30 minutes. Transfer to the fridge to chill for 3–4 hours.

Meanwhile, make the blueberry topping. Put the blueberries, sugar, lemon juice and 100ml of water in a pan, place over a medium heat and slowly bring to the boil. Mix the cornflour to a paste with a tablespoon of water, add this to the blueberries and cook for a couple of minutes until the mixture starts to thicken. Leave to cool fully and then refrigerate.

Run a sharp knife around the edge of the tin to loosen the cheesecake, then slide it on to a plate. Spread the blueberry topping over the top of the cheesecake or slice the cake and spoon some of the blueberry mixture over each portion. Serve immediately.

Surely there isn't anyone who doesn't love chocolate brownies? But, as I noticed in one of my favourite cookery books, *Completely Perfect* by Felicity Cloake, there's a deal of dissension about whether a perfect brownie should be fudgy or cakey. Being a middle of the road sort of person, I like a bit of both. So, I put masses of chocolate into my recipe, but I add cocoa powder as well which slightly cuts the richness, but not the squidginess, and creates the crust. The other thing is that I don't use butter but prefer sunflower oil, which I think gives the brownie a unique flavour and mouth feel. I always throw in some chunks of chocolate for texture and sometimes I add chopped walnuts or dried cherries or cranberries. I only recall brownies from about the last fifteen years, so for me they seem like a very late arrival from the USA. They hail from the Palmer House hotel in Chicago where they were first made in 1893. The hotel is still there and still serves brownies.

FUDGY CHOCOLATE BROWNIES

MAKES 12–16

150g dark chocolate
   (70% cocoa solids),
   broken up
190ml sunflower oil
250g caster sugar
3 eggs, lightly beaten
2 tsp vanilla extract
110g plain flour
   (regular or gluten-free)
40g cocoa powder
½ tsp salt
75g white or dark or
   milk chocolate chunks

Preheat the oven 180°C/Fan 160°C. Grease a baking tin, about 20 x 25cm in size, and line the base with baking parchment.

Put the dark chocolate into a heatproof bowl, set it over a pan of simmering water and leave until melted.

In a large bowl, whisk together the sunflower oil and caster sugar until well combined. Add the beaten eggs and vanilla extract, then stir in the melted chocolate. Sift in the plain flour, cocoa powder and salt, then stir to combine. Stir in the chocolate chunks.

Pour the glossy batter into the prepared tin and bake in the centre of the oven for 22–25 minutes. There should be a crust on top and the mixture should have lost its wobble. Remove from the oven and leave to cool in the tin.

When completely cool, cut into squares or bars. Serve or store in an airtight tin for 4–5 days. If desired, the brownies can be warmed in a microwave for 20–30 seconds and served with ice cream.

I don't know if I really need to say that flapjacks are one of the nation's favourite sweet traybakes. You only need to walk into any of the café chains and you'll see them on the counter with the chocolate brownies. This is a plain classic version, but you can mix in a handful of raisins, walnuts, chopped apricots, sunflower and pumpkin seeds or some chopped preserved ginger with the oats if the fancy takes you.

FLAPJACKS MAKES 12 BARS

160g butter
125g demerara or
    brown soft sugar
4 tbsp golden syrup
Good pinch of salt
250g jumbo or rolled oats

Line a 20 x 20cm square tin with baking parchment, making sure it goes up the sides of the tin. Preheat the oven to 180°C/Fan 160°C.

In a large pan, melt the butter, then add the sugar, golden syrup and salt. Stir over a low heat until well combined. Stir in the oats and mix well so they are thoroughly coated in the buttery mixture. Use a spatula to scrape the mixture into the lined tin, then pat down to smooth the top. Bake for about 20–22 minutes until golden.

Allow the flapjacks to cool and set in the tin for about 30 minutes, then lift them out with the parchment and cut into 12 bars.

What constitutes a perfect scone? I think it's a combination of heaviness and lightness. This recipe has got plenty of flour and butter but also a double quantity of bicarb of soda – first in the self-raising flour and second in that I have added extra baking powder. The result is a scone that tastes almost like soda water. It's also slightly on the salty side and brings out the best in jam and also cream. There's an expression, 'the sweet spot', which to me is when opposing forces are held in check with each other and it's a very important part of good cooking. I think this recipe has it.

SCONES MAKES 8

325g self-raising flour,
    plus extra for dusting
Pinch of salt
2 tsp baking powder
85g butter, cubed,
    at room temperature
1 tbsp caster sugar
175–200ml milk, at room
    temperature, plus extra
    for glazing

To serve
Raspberry or strawberry jam
Clotted or whipped cream

Preheat the oven to 220°C/Fan 200°C.

In a large bowl, sift the flour with the salt and baking powder. Add the cubed butter and rub it in until the mixture resembles breadcrumbs. Stir in the caster sugar.

Make a dip in the centre, add 175ml of the milk and use a knife to bring the mixture together into a dough. Add a little more milk if needed. Tip the dough out on to a floured surface and dust the top with a little flour. Use your hands to press the dough into a rough circle about 4–5cm thick.

With a 5cm cutter, stamp out 8 rounds. Try not to twist the cutter, as straight cuts give a better rise. You may need to re-form the dough to make the last couple of scones.

Straight away, transfer the scones to a lightly floured baking tray and brush the tops with milk. Bake for 10–12 minutes, until well risen and golden on top. Allow to cool a little, then serve with jam and cream.

TIP
If you want to make these in advance, pack them in plastic bags once cooled, then freeze. To serve, defrost at room temperature, then pop them in a 150°C/Fan 130°C oven for a few minutes to refresh.

The Victoria sandwich epitomises the very best in British cakes; like a simple Italian dish there are not too many notes in this classic – just the amount required, to paraphrase Mozart in *Amadeus*. You can, of course, go a little bit further and add some whipped cream or pastry cream to the filling but for me, just jam is best.

VICTORIA SANDWICH SERVES 8

230g butter, at room temperature, plus extra for greasing
230g golden caster sugar
4 eggs, at room temperature, beaten
230g self-raising flour
1 tsp baking powder
1 tsp vanilla extract
1 tbsp milk (if needed)
½ jar of good-quality raspberry jam (or strawberry if you prefer)
150ml double cream, whipped or buttercream if preferred (optional)
Icing sugar, for dusting

Preheat the oven to 180°C/Fan 160°C. Grease 2 x 20cm sandwich tins with butter and line the bases with baking parchment.

Put the soft butter and caster sugar in a large bowl and beat with an electric whisk until light and fluffy. Start adding the beaten eggs a little at a time – if the mixture starts to curdle, add a teaspoon of flour and continue. Sift in the rest of the flour and the baking powder and fold them in gently. Add the vanilla extract and milk, if needed, to make a soft, spoonable mixture.

Divide the batter between the 2 tins. Make a slight depression in the centre of each so that the cakes come out level, then bake for 25 minutes. The cakes should have slightly shrunk away from the sides, be springy to the touch and a skewer poked into the sponge should come out clean.

Transfer the cakes to a wire rack and allow them to cool in their tins for 5 minutes. Run a butter or palette knife around the tin to loosen, then turn the cakes out on to a wire rack to cool completely.

Place one sponge upside down on a plate and smother with plenty of jam – and cream or buttercream, if using. Place the second sponge on top with the browned side uppermost. Dust the top with some icing sugar and serve.

Much as I love sourdough, I am inordinately fond of very simple, mass-produced soft white rolls straight out of the oven. These cinnamon rolls are of exactly the same consistency, albeit with a little sugar added and a filling of butter, sugar and cinnamon. I love those cinnamon swirls made with puff pastry like a Danish, but these soft voluminous rolls are more than a match for them. They are best eaten the day they are made, with a cup of coffee or tea.

CINNAMON ROLLS MAKES 12

400g plain flour, plus extra for dusting
50g caster sugar
Pinch of salt
7g sachet of fast-action dried yeast
185ml tepid milk
50g butter, at room temperature
1 tsp vanilla extract
1 large egg, beaten

Filling
70g very soft butter
70g brown soft sugar
1 heaped tbsp ground cinnamon

Icing
100g icing sugar, sifted
1 tsp vanilla extract

Put the flour, caster sugar, salt and yeast in the bowl of a large stand mixer. In a small pan, warm the milk and butter to about blood temperature (37–40°C).

Add the milk and butter to the flour mixture, then the vanilla and beaten egg. Use a paddle beater or dough hook to mix to a soft dough. Up the speed slightly and then knead the dough for about 4 minutes until it is soft and elastic. If it's very sticky, add a little more flour to form a non-sticky, soft dough. Turn off the mixer and let the dough rest for 15 minutes. You can, of course, knead the dough by hand if you don't have a stand mixer.

In a small bowl, mix the filling ingredients together until they are well combined.

On a lightly floured surface, roll out the dough to form a rectangle about 40 x 25cm. Spread the filling over the dough, then roll into a Swiss roll shape to make a 40cm log. Cut this log into 12 slices.

Take a tin measuring roughly 23 x 33cm in size and line it with a large sheet of baking parchment. Arrange the rolls of dough, cut-side up, leaving space around each one as they will expand to fill the gaps. Cover with a clean tea towel and leave to rise in a warm place for 1–1½ hours until doubled in bulk.

Preheat the oven to 190°C/Fan 170°C. When the rolls have risen, bake them for about 25 minutes until risen and golden. Transfer them, still in the tin, to cool on a wire rack.

When the rolls are cool, mix the icing sugar and vanilla extract with 3 teaspoons of water. Drizzle the icing over the whole batch.

THE FUTURE OF FARMING?

Do you think strawberries all year round are a good thing? Normally, I would say no, things should be in their season, but I do remember Keith Floyd once saying when he owned a restaurant in Provence that seasonality was all very well and good until you'd had nothing but green flageolet beans for three weeks. Generally, like most people, I've always assumed that the sort of strawberries or tomatoes you get in the middle of winter that have been grown a long way off and transported for many days are not worth bothering with. Suppose, though, those strawberries were a great flavoursome variety, were grown in climate-controlled conditions with heating that is self-sufficient, and were delivered to the supermarket overnight within twenty-four hours of being picked – no airmiles? I wonder if you could be persuaded to change your mind? This is what Sir James Dyson is doing in his fifteen-acre greenhouse in Lincolnshire.

The berries are grown hydroponically – without soil – which you may disapprove of, but Dyson argues that the variety of strawberry is far more important for sweetness, flavour and juiciness than the growing method. He uses almost no fertiliser, hardly any chemicals and no pesticides, relying instead on releasing other insects to kill any pests. The energy needed to power and heat all of this is created by growing green crops, composting them and feeding the liquid created into a digester which converts the rich liquid into power.

Apart from a slight feeling of being caught between a Fritz Lang movie and *Brave New World*, I did understand the possibilities for this type of farming generally, but I pointed out that you would need a frightful lot of money to set something like this up. I had to concede that the technology, though massively expensive at the outset, could be of benefit in the future when the costs come down, and I've noted when filming in other parts of the country that farmers are already using digesters to produce fertiliser.

Before I arrived at the Dyson farm I'd heard that all the strawberry picking was done by robots. In fact, there are only a handful of them operating so far, but you can see by their quiet, slow, methodical precision and how they know the ripe from the unripe berries the way things are heading.

Naturally I had some reservations about this style of growing and harvesting. I couldn't help thinking about the fabulous lunches enjoyed by grape pickers in Burgundy, where they feast on things like duck parmentier, a sort of French cottage pie made with duck, which they wash down with lots of young Pinot Noir, and the olive pickers in

'Apart from a slight feeling of being caught between a Fritz Lang movie and Brave New World, I did understand the possibilities for this type of farming generally'

Greece picnicking under the trees. Picking is hard work, true, but do we want to lose that human interaction?

So, thank goodness for Kent, the garden of England, where the vast majority of the UK's cherries are grown. We filmed at Little Sharsted Farm where all the cherries are still picked by hand. The pickers stand on ladders and still use old-fashioned wicker baskets round their waists to collect the fruit. The contrast with the Dyson farm is almost like comparing one of the Patrick O'Brian naval ships with the spaceship in 2001.

The taste of those cherries, which only have an eight-week picking season and are so much a part of the English summer when they are here, was wonderful. Cherries are a passion of mine, and these were the darkest, largest and juiciest and sweetest I've ever tasted. As I picked and ate the glorious fruit straight from the trees, I thought of the poem by Robert Herrick:

Cherry-ripe, ripe, ripe, I cry,
Full and fair ones; come and buy:
If so be you ask me where
They do grow? I answer, there
Where my Julia's lips do smile; –
There's the land, or cherry-isle,
Whose plantations fully show
All the year where cherries grow.

Robert Herrick, 'Hesperides', 1648

This simple and delightful dessert comes from a little restaurant near Toulouse, but I cooked it for my TV series after a visit to James Dyson's strawberry farm, near Boston in Lincolnshire. You'll find more about this on page 234, but the object of his high-tech methods is to produce strawberries all year round. Whatever you personally feel about this, there is a massive market for them and I had to admit the berries were really good as well as being ecologically sound. They made a perfect sorbet.

STRAWBERRY SORBET SERVES 4

150g sugar
500g fresh ripe strawberries, hulled
Juice of a lemon

To serve
Langue du chat biscuits
   (see p.266)
Crème Chantilly (see p.270)
Extra strawberries, sliced

Put the sugar in a pan with 300ml of water and stir over a medium heat until the sugar has fully dissolved. Bring to the boil and boil for 5–6 minutes until you have a viscous syrup. Remove from the heat and leave to cool completely.

Put the strawberries in a blender or food processor with the lemon juice and blitz to form a smooth purée. Combine the purée with the cooled syrup and pour the mixture into an ice cream machine. Churn until soft set, then transfer to a plastic box, cover with a lid and freeze for 3–4 hours until ready to serve.

If you don't have an ice cream machine, combine the purée and syrup as above, pour into a plastic box and put it in the freezer for about an hour or until the mixture is starting to freeze. Use a fork to break up the ice crystals, then put the mixture back in the freezer for another hour. Repeat 2 or 3 times more, then freeze until set.

Before serving, let the sorbet soften slightly in the fridge for 10–15 minutes so it's easier to scoop. Serve with biscuits, crème Chantilly and sliced strawberries.

There are few people who would doubt the popularity of banoffee pie as a favourite dessert. It has all the hallmarks of being American, but it was invented in 1971 at The Hungry Monk restaurant in Sussex – sadly, now closed down. I remember being slightly snooty about a pudding with the name banoffee until I tasted it. The only difference between this and the standard recipe is the addition of a tablespoon or two of rum, which does seem to me to give a touch of added intrigue.

BANOFFEE PIE SERVES 6–8

Base
220g digestive biscuits
130g butter, melted

Filling
75g butter
75g brown soft sugar
397g tin of condensed milk
Pinch of salt

To finish
30g butter
1 tbsp brown soft sugar
3 firm bananas, sliced
2 tbsp rum, plus extra
   if desired
200ml double cream
20g dark chocolate,
   grated or chocolate
   flake, crumbled

Put the digestive biscuits in a plastic bag and crush them with a rolling pin or a wooden spoon. Melt the 130g butter in a pan and stir in the biscuit crumbs.

Press the buttery crumbs into a 20cm loose-bottomed cake tin, covering the base and sides, like a pastry case. Chill this in the freezer for 10 minutes while you make the filling.

Melt the 75g of butter in a pan and add the brown sugar, condensed milk and salt, then stir to combine. Bring to the boil and boil rapidly for a minute or so until the mixture is a deep golden colour, stirring continuously to prevent it sticking and burning on the bottom of the pan. Pour into the chilled case, allow to cool and then chill in the fridge for an hour.

Rinse out the pan and heat the 30g of butter and tablespoon of brown sugar, stirring until they are combined. Add the sliced bananas and fry until golden and coated in the butter and sugar. Drizzle over the rum and allow it to bubble up, then set aside to cool.

Arrange the bananas over the caramel in the tart case. Lightly whip the cream, adding extra rum if desired, and smooth it over the bananas, then top with grated or crumbled chocolate. Chill until ready to serve.

In the eighties we used to sell a large number of seafood pancakes at The Seafood Restaurant and as a result I became pretty good at making them. I would work with two pans and it became very easy to make a lot of pancakes, all of them perfect. I also love all sweet fillings for pancakes, but lemon and sugar are what we always had on Shrove Tuesday when I was a child.

PANCAKES WITH LEMON & SUGAR SERVES 4–6

125g plain flour
Pinch of salt
1 egg, beaten
300ml milk
1 tbsp oil, plus extra
   for cooking

To serve
Caster sugar
2–3 lemons,
   cut into wedges

Whisk the flour, salt, egg, milk and tablespoon of oil together in a bowl to make a smooth batter. Set aside for a few minutes to rest.

Heat a 20cm non-stick frying or crêpe pan over a medium heat. Swirl in a little oil and pour out any excess – the pan should be just coated not swimming in oil. Pour in enough batter to coat the bottom of the pan evenly and after about a minute or so, use a palette knife to loosen the edges and flip the pancake over to cook the other side. Remove, place on a warm plate and cover with a tea towel. Continue to cook and stack up the pancakes until all the batter is used.

Sprinkle with caster sugar and serve warm with lemon wedges.

My wife Sas loves what she calls a bombe Alaska which I believe is a baked Alaska with brandy poured over it and set alight. She likes dishes like this and crêpes suzette that involve some excitement and theatre, mainly because as a child she used to be taken to a smart restaurant in Sydney where they served such desserts. I agree there's something quite special about a dish with caramelised meringue on the outside and still frozen ice cream on the inside. I used to make baked Alaska in the early days of The Seafood Restaurant. Customers, maybe a little tipsy, would think that the core of ice cream would surely melt when put in a very hot oven and couldn't believe it would work. I'd explain that the meringue acts as an insulating blanket for the ice cream.

BAKED ALASKA SERVES 12

1 litre raspberry ripple
   or vanilla ice cream
   (or a mixture)
4 tbsp raspberry jam
Fresh raspberries, to serve

Sponge
100g butter, at room
   temperature, plus
   extra for greasing
100g caster sugar
2 eggs, beaten
100g self-raising flour
½ tsp baking powder
1 tsp vanilla extract

Meringue
4 egg whites
225g caster sugar

Allow the ice cream to soften a little, then transfer it to a small (1-litre) Pyrex bowl, pressing it down and smoothing the surface. Cover and put the bowl of ice cream in the freezer to refreeze and create a dome.

For the sponge, preheat the oven to 180°C/Fan 160°C. Grease a 20cm sandwich cake tin with butter and line it with baking parchment. Whisk the butter and sugar together in a bowl until creamy, then add the eggs a little at a time until all incorporated. If the mixture starts to curdle, add a teaspoon of the flour. Fold in the rest of the flour and the baking powder, then stir in the vanilla extract.

Scrape the mixture into the tin and bake for 20 minutes until golden and well risen. Transfer the cake to a wire rack and leave to cool fully. You can prepare to this stage the day before you want to serve the pudding.

Put the cooled sponge on a baking tray and spread it with the jam. Unmould the ice cream by dipping the bowl briefly in hot water, then running a knife around edge to loosen. Turn the ice cream dome on to the sponge and transfer to the freezer for 30–60 minutes.

For the meringue, whisk the egg whites in a clean, grease-free bowl. When the mixture is white and fluffy, increase the mixer speed and add the caster sugar a spoonful at a time until it is all incorporated and the mixture looks thick and glossy. Preheat the oven to 240°C/Fan 220°C.

Remove the sponge and ice cream from the freezer. Using a spatula, cover them with meringue, then swirl it attractively. Place in the preheated oven for 3–4 minutes until golden, then serve immediately with some fresh raspberries. (If you have a blowtorch, you could use that to brown the meringue instead of putting it in the oven.)

There's no question that rice pudding is still as popular as it has ever been. I love it and for me it should have a slightly firm texture but not be too creamy. It's not as rich as something like a crème brûlée which is all cream, and I think that a nice rice pudding with a burnt caramel top is almost better than a crème brûlée for that reason.

RICE PUDDING BRÛLÉE SERVES 6

125g pudding rice
800ml whole milk
200ml double cream
1 vanilla pod, split or
   1 tsp vanilla extract
30g butter (optional)
65g caster sugar

Caramel topping
1 tbsp granulated sugar
   per pot

Put the rice, milk, cream and vanilla pod, if using, in a saucepan and bring to simmering point. Then turn down the heat and leave to cook for 30–40 minutes. At this point, the rice should be tender and still a bit soupy – it will thicken quite a bit on cooling.

Remove the vanilla pod, if you've added one, or if using vanilla extract, add it now together with the sugar and the butter, if using. Stir until the sugar has fully dissolved.

Divide between 6 ramekins (about 10cm diameter x 5cm deep). Leave to cool, but don't refrigerate, unless making a day ahead.

Add a tablespoon of granulated sugar to each ramekin. Grill under a very hot grill, or use a blowtorch, until the sugar has melted and caramelised to form a hard crackable layer.

There are more recipes for trifle than you can shake a stick at. I've written a couple myself in the past, one using Madeira cake back at a time when I thought that fruit in a trifle was too much. 'I prefer my trifle without fruit,' I wrote. 'I find the combination of a good, sandy sponge lightly soaked with a really good sherry, home-made custard and some whipped cream is enough.' I've changed my mind since then and find that some acidic fruit provides a pleasing contrast to the creaminess. For this trifle, I'm using frozen berries and a very light genoise-type sponge, which is very easy to make. Feel free, of course, to buy a ready-made sponge and indeed custard. This much-loved dish with its name meaning something not serious – even rather insignificant – is a lovely bit of British understatement, I think.

SHERRY TRIFLE WITH FROZEN BERRIES SERVES 8–12

Sponge
Butter, for greasing
3 eggs
85g caster sugar
85g self-raising flour
Pinch of salt

Trifle custard
400ml whole milk
300ml double cream
3 egg yolks
40g cornflour
45g caster sugar
½ tsp vanilla extract
Pinch of salt

To assemble
75ml good sherry,
    such as Oloroso
5 tbsp raspberry jam
400g frozen berries, defrosted
1 tbsp caster sugar
300ml double cream
20g flaked almonds
20g pomegranate seeds,
    if available, or 10g dried
    apricots, sliced, and 10g
    dried cranberries

First make the sponge. Preheat the oven to 190°C/Fan 170°C and grease a 20cm cake tin with butter.

Whisk the eggs with the caster sugar until pale and creamy. Sift over the flour and salt and carefully fold them in to retain as much air and lightness as possible. Pour the batter into the cake tin and bake for 20–25 minutes until risen and golden. Remove from the oven and leave to cool.

For the custard, bring the milk and cream to the boil. Beat the egg yolks, cornflour, sugar, vanilla extract and salt together in a bowl, then gradually whisk in the hot milk and cream. Return the mixture to the pan and place over a low heat, then cook, stirring constantly, for about 5 minutes until the mixture has thickened. Take care not to let it boil or it will curdle. Transfer the custard to a bowl, place a piece of scrunched greaseproof paper on the surface to prevent a skin forming, then leave to cool.

When ready to assemble, cut the sponge to fit the base of your chosen glass dish; if you use a 20cm dish the sponge will fit perfectly. Douse the sponge with the sherry. Warm the raspberry jam slightly and smooth it over the sponge, then scatter over the defrosted berries. Top with the cooled thick custard.

Add the tablespoon of caster sugar to the cream, then whip the cream to soft peaks. Spoon the cream over the custard and chill the trifle until ready to serve. Lightly toast the almonds in a dry frying pan, then scatter them over just before serving along with the pomegranate seeds or apricots and cranberries.

A proper old-fashioned fruit pie. The reason for having both Bramleys and Cox's apples in the filling is that Cox's keep their shape while the Bramleys fall apart but add a nice tartness and plenty of moisture to the pie.

DOUBLE-CRUST APPLE PIE WITH A TOUCH OF CINNAMON

SERVES 6

Pastry
350g plain flour, plus
    extra for dusting
Pinch of salt
125g cold butter, cubed
50g cold lard, cubed
A few tbsp very cold water
A little milk, to seal and glaze
1 tbsp caster or demerara
    sugar, to decorate

Filling
600g Bramley (cooking)
    apples, peeled and sliced
400g Cox's (eating) apples,
    peeled and sliced
About 2 tbsp caster sugar
20g butter
½ tsp ground cinnamon or
    ground cloves (optional)

To serve
Custard (see p.270)

You will need a pie dish about
    24–25cm in diameter.

To make the pastry, put the flour and salt in the bowl of a food processor and add the cubed butter and lard. Pulse until the mixture resembles breadcrumbs. Alternatively, mix in a large bowl, using your fingertips to rub the fat into the flour. Add the water, a tablespoon at a time until the pastry just starts to come together. You may not need all the water and less is more to achieve a nice short pastry. Tip out on to a lightly floured surface and bring the mixture together, then divide it into 2 balls, roughly two-thirds and one-third. Flatten each one slightly, then wrap and leave to rest in the fridge until ready to use.

Put the apples into a pan with the sugar and butter. Add a tablespoon of water and cover the pan, then cook over a medium heat for about 10 minutes until the Bramleys have broken down and the Cox slices are tender. If the mixture looks watery, cook without a lid for a couple of minutes to evaporate the excess liquid. Taste and add more sugar if required, then stir in the spice, if using. Tip the mixture into a bowl and leave to cool to room temperature.

Preheat the oven to 200°C/Fan 180°C. Put a heavy baking sheet on the middle shelf to preheat.

Roll out the larger disc of pastry to fit the bottom and sides of your pie dish with a small overhang, then add the cooled filling. Dampen the edges of the pastry with a little milk. Roll out the remaining pastry, then lay it over the filling. Press the pastry edges together, then crimp with your fingers or use a fork around the edges of the dish to seal. If you like, use any pastry scraps to make pastry leaves to decorate the top.

Use a sharp knife to cut a couple of slits in the centre to allow steam to escape. Brush the top with milk and sprinkle with sugar. Put the pie in the oven on the baking sheet and bake for about 30–35 minutes until the pastry is golden and crisp. Allow the pie to cool a little before cutting and serving with custard. *Recipe photographs overleaf.*

In the Glasgow episode of *Food Stories*, we celebrated the Italian diaspora and the fact that many families that came to live in the city in the late nineteenth and early twentieth centuries started ice cream parlours. We found a café called The University Café which was opened by Pasquale Verrecchia in 1918 and is still run by the family. I had a knickerbocker glory while talking about Italians in Glasgow and it was a treat sitting in one of the booths surrounded by 1950s' nostalgia.

KNICKERBOCKER GLORY SERVES 4

Strawberry sauce
250g strawberries
    (fresh or frozen)
40g sugar
Juice of ¼ lemon

Sundae
12 fresh strawberries,
    hulled and quartered
100g fresh raspberries
Handful of blueberries
500–600ml (about 8 scoops)
    ice cream of your choice
    – vanilla, raspberry ripple,
    clotted cream, etc.
100ml double cream, whipped
    (optional) or use Chantilly
    cream from a can
4 fan wafers or 8 café curls
Chocolate shavings,
    sprinkles, chopped
    pistachios (optional)

You will need 4 tall glasses
    and long-handled spoons.

Start with the strawberry sauce. Put all the ingredients in a pan and simmer for about 5 minutes until the strawberries have softened. Use a wooden spoon to push the strawberries through a sieve to remove the seeds. Set aside to cool, then refrigerate until needed.

Divide some of the fresh berries between your glasses. Top with a scoop of ice cream and drizzle over some of the cooled sauce. Top with more fruit and finish with a second scoop of ice cream. Drizzle over more of the sauce, then pipe on some whipped cream or add Chantilly cream.

Add a wafer or café curls and decorate with your choice of toppings. Serve immediately.

For me, bread and butter is a favourite nursery pudding. It was originally intended to use up stale bread and with that thought in mind, I think that simple white bread is the right choice for this recipe. Some people choose brioche or some other enriched dough, but I prefer the simple plainness of the bread with the creamy vanilla voluptuousness of the custard. I like to add some sultanas or candied peel or both to my bread and butter pudding and finish it with an apricot glaze, having first caramelised the top with icing sugar under the grill.

CARAMELISED BREAD & BUTTER PUDDING WITH SULTANAS & APRICOT GLAZE

SERVES 6–8

50g butter, plus extra
  for greasing
6–7 thin slices of white
  bread, crusts removed
100g sultanas or candied
  peel or a mixture
250ml double cream
250ml whole milk
3 medium eggs
50g caster sugar
1 vanilla pod
25g icing sugar
25g apricot jam,
  warmed and sieved

To serve
Clotted cream (optional)

Preheat the oven to 190°C/Fan 170°C. Butter a 1.5-litre shallow ovenproof dish – something about 6cm deep is ideal. Generously spread the slices of bread with butter and cut each slice into 4 triangles. Arrange a layer of the bread over the base of the dish, then sprinkle in the sultanas and/or candied peel. Arrange the remaining bread triangles on top.

Mix the cream, milk, eggs and sugar together and pass the mixture through a sieve. Slit open the vanilla pod, scrape out the seeds and whisk them into the custard. Pour the custard over the bread and leave to soak for 5 minutes.

Place the dish in a roasting tin and pour enough hot water into the tin to come halfway up the sides of the dish. Bake in the preheated oven for about 30 minutes, until the top is golden and the custard has lightly set but is still quite soft in the centre. Remove the dish from the roasting tin and leave to cool for about 15 minutes. Meanwhile, preheat the grill to its highest setting.

Generously dust the top of the pudding with icing sugar and place under the grill to glaze – watch it carefully, though, as it burns easily. If the top starts to puff up, remove the dish from the grill and let it cool a little longer before returning to the heat. Brush the top with the sieved apricot jam and serve with some clotted cream, if you wish.

When I was cooking these for the TV series I said they should be as light as clouds. I've just cooked them again and indeed they are. I think the three most important aspects of perfect profiteroles are great chocolate, eating them when just cooled down out of the oven, and no sugar in the whipped cream – just a little vanilla. This seems to accentuate the complexity of a good chocolate sauce.

PROFITEROLES WITH DARK CHOCOLATE SAUCE MAKES 16–20 PROFITEROLES

75g plain flour
Pinch of salt
55g cold butter,
    cut into small cubes
2 eggs, beaten

Chocolate sauce
30g butter
125g dark chocolate
    (70% cocoa solids),
    broken up

Filling
300ml double cream
1 tsp vanilla extract

Sift the flour and salt into a bowl. Put the butter in a pan with 150ml of water and place over a medium heat – ideally you want the water to come to the boil just as the butter has melted. Turn off the heat as soon as the water comes to the boil, then dump all the flour into the pan in one go. Vigorously beat in the flour to make a thick, lump-free paste. It should form a ball that leaves the sides of the pan clean. Use an electric whisk to do this if you like.

Transfer the mixture to a plate and leave it to cool for 10–15 minutes, then put it back into the cool pan or a bowl. Beat in the eggs, a little at a time, fully incorporating each addition before adding more. Continue until all the egg is used up and you have a smooth, glossy paste. Preheat the oven to 200°C/Fan 180°C.

Line a baking sheet with baking parchment and sprinkle it with a few drops of water. Using a piping bag, squeeze blobs of the paste on to the baking sheet, allowing space around them as they will puff up during cooking. The mixture should yield 16–20 profiteroles.

Bake the profiteroles for 10 minutes, then increase the heat to 220°C/Fan 200°C and cook for a further 15 minutes or so until they are well risen and golden. Pierce the base of each and make a small hole the size of a piping nozzle. Put the profiteroles back in the oven for 2 minutes, holes uppermost, to allow the insides to dry out a little. Then transfer them to a wire rack to cool.

For the sauce, place a heatproof bowl over a pan of just simmering water – the base of the bowl shouldn't touch the water. Add the butter and chocolate, then stir together until melted and smooth and glossy. Add a splash of water if the sauce seems too thick.

Whisk the cream and add the vanilla. Spoon the cream into a piping bag, fitted with a 0.5–1cm plain nozzle, and fill each profiterole. Serve the profiteroles drizzled with warm chocolate sauce.

This is in memory of a popular ice cream in the seventies: rum and raisin. I actually hated it because there was never any actual rum in it, just an unpleasant rum flavour. I did think of including a recipe for my own rum and raisin ice cream in this book, but I do think the combination is better in a classic sponge pudding, made with tea-soaked raisins, brown sugar, ginger, pecan nuts and rum, served with a rum-laced sauce.

RUM & RAISIN PUDDING WITH BUTTERSCOTCH SAUCE

MAKES 9 SQUARES

125g butter, diced, plus
  extra for greasing
150g raisins
200ml black tea or water
50ml dark rum
175g brown soft sugar
2 large eggs, beaten
225g plain flour
½ tsp bicarbonate of soda
Pinch of salt
1 tsp ground ginger
50g pecan nuts, chopped
  (optional)

Butterscotch sauce
100g unsalted butter, diced
200ml double cream
125g brown soft sugar
50ml dark rum

Grease a baking tin measuring about 22–23cm square and line it with baking parchment.

Put the raisins and tea or water in a pan and bring to the boil. Continue to cook for a minute, then take the pan off the heat and add the butter. Stir until the butter has melted, then add the rum.

Preheat the oven to 200°C/Fan 180°C. Allow the raisin mix to cool to blood temperature, then tip it into a large bowl and add the sugar and beaten eggs. Stir well, then add the dry ingredients and the nuts, if using, and fold together until well combined.

Pour into the prepared tin and bake for about 30 minutes until the sponge is springy and a skewer comes out clean. Leave to cool for 5–10 minutes while you make the sauce.

Put the butter, cream and sugar in a pan and place it over a medium heat until combined, then simmer for 5 minutes. Take the pan off the heat and stir in the rum.

Cut the sponge into 9 squares and serve warm with some of the butterscotch sauce poured over the top.

When I filmed at Bury Market, I was lucky enough to be able to taste chorley cakes and eccles cakes side by side. I realised that they are pretty much the same, but chorley cakes are made with shortcrust pastry and eccles cakes with puff. Chorley cakes are also less sweet, without the sugary topping of an eccles cake. They're traditionally eaten spread with a little butter and with a slice of Lancashire cheese on the side.

CHORLEY CAKES MAKES 8

Pastry
300g plain flour,
    plus extra for dusting
1 tsp baking powder
Pinch of salt
20g caster sugar
180g cold butter,
    cut into cubes
5 tbsp cold milk

Filling
200g currants
40g light brown soft sugar
50g butter, melted

Sift the flour, baking powder, salt and caster sugar into a bowl. Rub in the butter with your fingertips or whizz in a food processor until the mixture resembles breadcrumbs. Add enough of the cold milk to bring the mixture together and form a dough, then cover and chill for 30 minutes in the fridge.

Mix together the currants, sugar and melted butter and set aside.

Preheat the oven to 190°C/Fan 170°C. Roll out the pastry dough on a lightly floured surface. Using a saucer, cut the dough into 8 discs, each 14–15cm in diameter. Divide the currant filling between the pastry rounds, placing it in the centre, then fold the pastry over to encase the filling, Turn the cake over to hide the seam and gently press with the palm of your hand to flatten slightly. Some of the currants will show through a little but that's fine. Cut a couple of slits in the top of each cake.

Transfer the cakes to a baking sheet and bake them in the preheated oven for 18–20 minutes. You don't want the cakes to take on too much colour.

Leave the cakes to cool to room temperature, before serving. Nice spread with a little butter.

SIDES
& BASICS

CHEESY LEEKS
Serves 6–8

Great with the roast topside on pages 208–9, or even on its own with a green salad.

50g butter, plus extra for greasing
500g trimmed leeks, sliced and well washed
50g plain flour
600ml milk
1 tsp Dijon mustard
125g mature Cheddar, grated
25g panko breadcrumbs
Salt and black pepper

Preheat the oven to 190°C/Fan 170°C.
Grease an oven dish about 20 x 25cm in size.

Melt the butter in a pan over a medium heat and add the leeks. Cook gently for about 5 minutes until the leeks have softened a little, then add the flour and stir over the heat for a minute before gradually adding the milk. Stir until the sauce starts to thicken, then add the mustard, bring to the boil and stir while the mixture continues to thicken.

Add all but 2 tablespoons of the grated cheese to the leeks and stir to melt. Taste and season with salt and plenty of black pepper.

Turn the leeks into the buttered dish, top with the panko crumbs mixed with the remaining cheese and grind over more black pepper. Bake for about 20 minutes until golden and bubbling.

GLAZED CARROTS WITH STAR ANISE
Serves 4

Serve with roast or grilled meat, such as the roast topside (pages 208–9).

450g carrots, cut on the diagonal into slices 1cm thick
   or use whole scrubbed baby carrots
½ tsp honey
15g butter
1 star anise
Salt and black pepper

Put the carrots in a pan and add 300–400ml of water, enough to barely cover them. Add the honey, butter and star anise, then season with salt and pepper. Cover with a tight-fitting lid and simmer until just tender.

Uncover the pan, increase the heat and boil rapidly to reduce the liquid. Shake the pan every now and then until just before the carrots start to catch on the base. Let the carrots colour very slightly here and there. Remove the star anise and toss well before serving.

ITALIAN-STYLE GREENS
Serves 4

A good side with any main dish.

20g butter
1 shallot, finely chopped
200g savoy cabbage, spring greens or kale, shredded
Small handful of parsley, chopped
Salt and black pepper

Heat the butter over a medium-high heat, add the shallot and fry for a few minutes until softened. Add the cabbage, cover the pan and allow the cabbage to wilt in the heat for a couple of minutes. Add the parsley, season with salt and pepper, then serve.

CHIP SHOP MUSHY PEAS
Serves 4

*Serve with the chips and curry sauce
on page 115.*

250g dried marrowfat peas
850ml hot water
2 tsp bicarbonate of soda

To cook
650ml hot water
2 tbsp malt vinegar
Salt, to taste

Soak the peas overnight in the hot water
with the bicarbonate of soda.

The following day, drain the peas and rinse
them well. Put them in a clean pan with the
650ml of hot water and bring to the boil.
Boil for 15–20 minutes, skimming and
discarding any foam and skins from the
surface. Then turn down the heat and
continue to cook slowly until you have
the desired mushy consistency. Stir in the
malt vinegar and season to taste with salt.

CREAMY WHITE BEANS
Serves 4

*I had a very enjoyable visit to Pam Brunton's
restaurant, Inver, on the shores of Loch Fyne.
We ate some splendid lamb served with these
creamy beans and some foraged vegetables,
and this is a simplified version of her bean
dish using canned beans – Pam uses dried
and soaked. She also uses Corra Linn cheese,
but good alternatives are Pecorino or
Manchego. Nice with lamb chops.*

2 x 400g tins of cannellini beans, drained
2 garlic cloves, chopped
1 tbsp olive oil
30g butter
50g sheep cheese, such as Pecorino or Manchego
1 tbsp lemon juice
Salt

Put the beans in a pan and barely cover with
water – about 150ml depending on the size
of the pan – then add the garlic and olive oil.
Bring to the boil, then turn the heat down
and simmer for 5–10 minutes.

At this point, start to stir the beans while
still on the heat. The beans will release starch
into the water and a few of them will break
up slightly, which will turn the mixture 'creamy'.

Add the butter and cheese and keep stirring
until they're incorporated. Add the lemon
juice and season with salt to taste and stir
again. If the beans are too stiff, add a little
water until you get a sloppy consistency,
like thick soup.

SWEET POTATO WEDGES
Serves 4–6

Serve with the chicken fajitas on page 142.

1kg sweet potatoes, peeled
60ml olive oil
1 tsp smoked paprika (pimentón)
A few thyme sprigs, leaves stripped
   from stalks
½ tsp garlic powder
Salt and black pepper

Preheat the oven to 210°C/Fan 190°C.

Cut the sweet potatoes in half lengthways, then into wedges. Toss the wedges in a bowl with the oil, paprika, thyme, garlic powder, salt and pepper until coated.

Spread them out on a large baking tray, then bake for 25–30 minutes until tender and golden. Serve immediately.

Delicious with a sriracha mayo dip made with 2 tablespoons of mayonnaise, 1 tablespoon of crème fraiche or yoghurt and 1 tablespoon of sriracha.

QUICK DAUPHINOISE POTATOES
Serves 4

The perfect accompaniment to a rack of lamb (see page 168).

900g floury potatoes, such
   as Maris Pipers, peeled
15g butter, for greasing
300ml double cream
300ml whole milk
1 garlic clove, crushed
Freshly grated nutmeg
Salt and black pepper

Preheat the oven to 200°C/Fan 180°C. Slice the potatoes very thinly by hand or using a mandoline or food processor. Lightly butter a 1.5 litre shallow ovenproof dish.

Put the cream, milk and garlic in a large non-stick saucepan and season with nutmeg, salt and pepper. Add the sliced potatoes and simmer for 10 minutes, stirring them very gently now and then so as not to break up the slices. They are ready once they are just tender when pierced with the tip of a sharp knife.

Spoon everything into the buttered dish, overlapping the top layer of potatoes neatly if you wish.

Bake in the oven for 20–25 minutes or until golden and bubbling. Leave to stand for 5–10 minutes before cutting and serving.

ROAST POTATOES
Serves 6–8

A roast dinner isn't complete without these.

1.75kg floury potatoes, such as Maris Pipers
   or King Edwards, peeled
250g goose or duck fat
Salt

Cut the potatoes into large chunks and put them in a pan of well-salted water (1 teaspoon of salt per 600ml). Bring to the boil and simmer for 8–10 minutes. Drain and leave in a colander to dry off. Preheat the oven to 220°C/Fan 200°C.

Meanwhile, put the fat in a large roasting tin in which the potatoes will fit in a single layer and place it in the oven for 5 minutes to heat.

Shake the potatoes in the colander to rough up the edges. Remove the roasting tin from the oven, add the potatoes and turn them over once or twice until well coated. Roast the potatoes for 50–60 minutes until crisp and golden.

SAUTÉED POTATOES
Serves 4

Good with the Dover sole on page 84.

700g floury potatoes, such as Maris Pipers
   or King Edwards, peeled
50g butter
3 tbsp olive oil
Salt and black pepper

Cut the potatoes into 2cm cubes, put them in a pan of well-salted water (1 teaspoon of salt per 600ml). Bring to the boil, then simmer until tender. Drain well and leave until the steam has died down and the potatoes have dried off a little.

Heat the butter and oil in a large, heavy-based frying pan. Add the potatoes and toss them repeatedly over a medium heat for 10 minutes until they are crisp, dry, sandy and light brown. The outside of the potatoes should break off a little as you sauté them to give them a nice crumbly crust.

To make sure the potatoes aren't too greasy, blot the pan with kitchen paper to remove any excess oil. Season at the last minute with salt and black pepper.

COLCANNON
Serves 4–6

Serve with the pot-roast brisket on page 198.

1kg floury potatoes, King Edwards
   or Maris Pipers, peeled
100g butter, at room temperature
200g savoy cabbage, or curly kale,
   finely shredded
100ml whole milk
Salt and black pepper

Cut the potatoes into chunks and put them in a pan of well-salted water (1 teaspoon of salt per 600ml). Boil for 15–20 minutes until tender, then drain well. In a separate pan, melt about a third of the butter over a medium heat and add the shredded cabbage. Cook for about 5 minutes until wilted.

Add the rest of the butter and the milk to the potatoes, then mash until smooth. Stir in the cabbage and season with salt and pepper.

POTATO SALAD
Serves 4–6

Nice with the sea trout on page 56.

1kg new potatoes, such as Jersey Royals, scrubbed
2 banana shallots, finely chopped
2 eggs, hard-boiled, peeled and chopped
1–2 tbsp capers
1–2 gherkins/dill pickles, finely chopped
4 tbsp olive oil
1 tbsp red wine or sherry vinegar
2 tbsp mayonnaise
Small handful of parsley or a mix of parsley
   and tarragon or dill, chopped
Salt and black pepper

Boil the potatoes in salted water (1 teaspoon of salt per 600ml), then drain and cool. Cut them into halves or quarters, depending on size, and mix with the remaining ingredients.

MANGO AND TOMATO SALAD
Serves 4

Good with the jerk chicken on page 146.

1 large mango, peeled and diced into 1cm pieces
15 cherry tomatoes, quartered
½ cucumber, diced into 1cm pieces
Handful of fresh coriander, chopped
Juice of 1 lime
½ scotch bonnet chilli, seeds removed,
   finely chopped
¼ tsp salt

It's best to make this salad just before serving or the fruit will start to get soggy. Simply prepare all the ingredients and combine in a bowl.

KOREAN CUCUMBER SALAD
Serves 4

Serve with the Korean fried chicken wings on page 148.

1 cucumber, sliced into rings
1 tbsp soy sauce
2 tbsp rice vinegar
1 tbsp caster sugar
½–¾ tsp gochugaru (Korean chilli powder)
   or ¼–½ tsp chilli flakes
½ tsp sesame seeds
2 spring onions, finely sliced on the diagonal

Combine the sliced cucumber in a bowl with the soy sauce, rice vinegar and caster sugar. Stir well, then add the gochugaru, starting with half a teaspoon (or quarter of a teaspoon of chilli flakes), and adjust to taste. Leave the salad to stand for 10 minutes, then just before serving, sprinkle over the sesame seeds and spring onions.

KOREAN LETTUCE SALAD
Serves 4

Serve with the Korean chicken on page 148.

250g soft lettuce leaves, such as oakleaf or little gem
½ red onion, finely sliced
2 spring onions, finely sliced
1 tbsp toasted sesame seeds
¼ tsp salt
1 tbsp gochugaru (Korean chilli powder)
    or 1 tsp chilli flakes

Dressing
3 tbsp soy sauce
2 tbsp rice vinegar
1 tsp clear honey

Mix the lettuce, red onion and spring onions in a bowl, then add the toasted sesame seeds, salt and the gochugaru or chilli flakes and toss well. For the dressing, mix the soy sauce, rice vinegar and honey with 2 tablespoons of water. Pour this over the spiced leaves and serve immediately.

EGG-FRIED RICE
Serves 3–4

Good with the Chinese chicken curry (see page 138) and sweet and sour pork (see page 184).

2 tbsp vegetable oil
4 spring onions, sliced, white and green parts separated
3 eggs, beaten
400g cooked long-grain rice (about 140g uncooked)
1 tbsp soy sauce

Heat the oil in a wok. Add the white parts of the spring onions and cook for a minute or so until softened a little, then add the beaten eggs and cook until almost scrambled. Pour in the rice and stir the grains to separate. Add the green parts of the onions and the soy sauce and stir until well combined.

KUBO AROMATIC JASMINE RICE
Serves 4

This is the recipe for the rice I ate at the Kubo stall in Bristol. Serve with the pork belly adobo on page 179.

300g jasmine rice
2–3 large garlic cloves
Vegetable oil
1 bay leaf
½ tbsp cracked black pepper
1 pandan leaf, fresh or frozen (optional)

Rinse the rice in a bowl of cold water at least 3 times until the water runs clear, then drain.

Peel and chop the garlic cloves, then put them in a pan with a little oil and fry until golden brown.

Add the rice to a saucepan and cover with 500ml of water. Add the bay leaf, black pepper, pandan leaf, if using, and the browned garlic. With your hands, stir the rice to incorporate the aromatics and to level off the rice in the water.

Place the pan over a medium-high heat, uncovered, and bring to a rolling boil. Once boiling, remove the pan from the heat, cover with a lid and set aside for 20–30 minutes by which time the rice should be cooked. Remove the lid and fluff up the rice with a fork before serving.

RICK'S EVERYDAY PILAU RICE
Serves 4

*Good with the chicken tikka masala
on page 134.*

1 tsp vegetable oil
2 cloves
3cm cinnamon stick
1 green cardamom pod, crushed
315g basmati rice
¼ tsp salt

Heat the oil in a saucepan and fry the spices
for 30 seconds until they smell aromatic.

Add the rice to the pan with the salt and
stir gently. Add 400ml of water and bring
to the boil, then cook over a very low heat
with the lid on for 10–12 minutes until all
the water has been absorbed.

BROWN RICE
Serves 4

Serve with the teriyaki salmon on page 54.

1 tbsp vegetable oil
350g brown rice
½ tsp salt

Heat the oil and fry the rice for 30 seconds.
Add 525ml of water and the salt, bring to
the boil, then turn the heat down to a low
simmer. Cook for 30 minutes with the lid on.

CHAPATIS
Makes 8

*Serve with the chicken tikka masala on page
134 or the lamb rogan josh on page 172.*

250g chapati flour, or 125g wholemeal and
    125g plain white flour, plus extra for dusting
½ tsp salt
2 tbsp melted ghee, butter or vegetable oil,
    plus extra for brushing
120–150ml warm water

In a bowl, mix the flour with the salt, then
add the melted ghee, butter or oil and 120ml
of the water. Mix together, adding a little
more water if needed, until you have a soft
but not sticky dough. Knead in the bowl for
a minute or two, then cover and leave to
rest for about 15 minutes.

Divide the dough into 8 pieces. On a lightly
floured surface, roll each piece into a ball,
then use a lightly floured rolling pin to roll
each piece out into a circle measuring about
13cm in diameter.

Heat a heavy-based frying pan or griddle
over a medium heat. When it's hot, place one
of the circles of dough in the pan and cook for
1–2 minutes, or until bubbles appear on the
surface and the bread puffs up. Flip the bread
over, press it down with a spatula so that it
cooks evenly, then cook for a further minute
or until golden-brown.

Remove from the pan and place on
a warm plate covered by a tea towel to
keep warm while you cook the rest.

Brush the chapatis with a little melted
ghee, butter or vegetable oil or leave plain.
Serve warm.

FLATBREADS
Makes 8

*Just right with the falafel on page 100
and the lamb kofta kebabs on page 173.*

500g strong flour, plus extra for rolling
7g sachet of fast-action dried yeast
Pinch of sugar
10g salt
275ml warm water
60ml olive oil, plus extra for greasing

Sift the flour into a large bowl and add
the yeast, sugar and salt. Make a well in the
centre and add the water and olive oil. Knead
on a floured surface, or in a food mixer with
a dough hook, for about 4 minutes until you
have a soft, elastic dough. Place in a clean,
lightly oiled bowl and cover with cling film.
Leave the dough to rise for 30–60 minutes
until doubled in bulk.

Preheat the oven to 230°C/Fan 210°C
and place a baking sheet in the oven to heat
up. Divide the dough into 8 pieces. Roll out
each piece on a lightly floured surface into
ovals or rounds of about 3mm thick. Bake
for 7–10 minutes – in batches if necessary –
until browned in spots. Serve immediately.

SHORTCRUST PASTRY
Makes 300g

A good basic pastry recipe for pies and tarts.

200g plain flour, plus extra for dusting
½ tsp salt
50g very cold butter, cubed
50g very cold lard, cubed
2 tbsp very cold water

Sift the flour and salt into a food processor
or a mixing bowl. Add the butter and lard and
pulse or work together with your fingers until
the mixture looks like coarse breadcrumbs.

Add enough water to bring everything
together into a dough, then turn out on to
a lightly floured surface. Shape the dough
into a disc about 4–5cm thick, then cover
and chill until ready to use.

LANGUES DE CHAT BISCUITS
Makes about 20

Just the thing to serve with the strawberry sorbets on page 236.

1 large egg white
50g unsalted butter, at room temperature
50g golden caster sugar
50g plain flour, sifted

Preheat the oven to 200°C/Fan 180°C. Line 2 baking trays with baking parchment.

Using electric beaters, whisk the egg white until frothy. In a separate bowl, beat the butter and sugar until pale, light and fluffy, then gradually whisk in the egg white. Once the egg white is incorporated, fold in the sifted flour.

Spoon the mixture into a piping bag fitted with a 1cm plain nozzle. Pipe stripes about 7–8cm long on to the baking trays, spacing them well as they will spread in the oven.

Bake for up to 7–8 minutes but check after 5 minutes. The biscuits should be golden around the edges. Leave them to cool on the trays for a few minutes before transferring them to a wire rack to cool completely. The biscuits can be stored in an airtight tin for a few days if necessary.

EVERYDAY MAYONNAISE
Makes 300ml

A good basic mayo, this can be kept in the fridge for at least two weeks.

1 whole egg or 2 egg yolks (see method)
2 tsp white wine vinegar
1 tsp hot English mustard or Dijon
¾ tsp salt
300ml sunflower oil

The simplest way to make this is to put a whole egg, the vinegar, mustard and salt in a food processor. Turn on the machine and very slowly trickle the oil through the hole in the lid until you have a thick emulsion.

To make the mayonnaise by hand, make sure all the ingredients are at room temperature and use 2 egg yolks, rather than a whole egg. Put the egg yolks, vinegar, mustard and salt into a mixing bowl and rest the bowl on a damp cloth to stop it moving around. Lightly whisk to break up the yolks and, using a wire whisk, beat in the oil, a few drops at a time, until it is all incorporated.

Once you have added the same volume of oil as the original mixture of egg yolks and vinegar, you can add the oil a little more quickly. This can be kept in the fridge for at least 2 weeks.

MUSTARD MAYONNAISE
Makes 300ml

This has a stronger mustard flavour than the everyday mayonnaise and is good for tartare sauce (see page 65) and dishes such as the prawn cocktail on page 32.

1 whole egg or 2 egg yolks (see method)
1 tbsp English mustard (made up, not powder)
1 tsp salt
1 tsp white wine vinegar
300ml sunflower oil

Blend the egg, mustard, salt and vinegar in a food processor. With the motor running, gradually add the oil in a slow trickle until it is all incorporated.

If making by hand, follow the method for the everyday mayonnaise opposite, using 2 egg yolks instead of a whole egg.

AIOLI
Makes about 175ml

Serve with the arroz roja on page 52 and the salt cod fishcakes on page 58.

4 garlic cloves, peeled
½ tsp salt
1 medium egg yolk
125ml sunflower oil
50ml extra virgin olive oil

Mash the garlic cloves to a paste with the salt, then scrape the garlic paste into a bowl and add the egg yolk. Whisk everything together, then very gradually whisk in the oil, a few drops at a time at first, to make a thick mayonnaise-like mixture.

CUCUMBER & MINT RAITA
Serves 8

Serve with the aubergine biryani on page 92.

175g unpeeled cucumber, halved lengthways
275g natural yoghurt
½ tsp caster sugar
3 tbsp chopped fresh mint leaves
1 tsp fresh lime juice
Salt and black pepper

Scoop out the seeds from the cucumber using a teaspoon, then grate the flesh. Toss the cucumber with a teaspoon of salt, tip it into a sieve and leave to drain for 20–30 minutes.

Mix the drained cucumber with all the remaining ingredients, adding a little extra salt, pepper or lime juice to taste. Eat this on the day of making.

HORSERADISH & APPLE SAUCE
Serves 8

Serve with the pot-roast brisket on page 198.

1 Bramley apple, peeled and chopped
2 tbsp creamed horseradish

Cook the apple in a splash of water for about 10 minutes until pulpy and broken down, then stir in the horseradish.

CHIPOTLES IN ADOBO SAUCE
Makes 1 x 370g jar

Useful for Mexican dishes, such as chilli con carne (see page 200).

8 chipotle chillies
150ml hot water
3 large ripe tomatoes, skinned and roughly chopped
1 medium onion, roughly chopped
4 large garlic cloves, peeled and sliced
60ml apple cider vinegar
¾ tsp salt
2 tsp brown sugar

Remove the hard stems from the chillies, but leave the seeds in. Place the chillies in a bowl and cover them with the hot water. Cover the bowl with cling film and leave the chillies to soak for about 20 minutes.

Remove 3 of the soaked chillies and set them aside. Put the rest of the chillies and the soaking liquid in a food processor or blender with the tomatoes, onion, garlic, apple cider vinegar, salt and sugar and process to make a smooth paste.

Tip the paste into a pan and add the remaining whole soaked chillies. Bring to the boil, then reduce the heat and simmer the chillies for up to an hour. Keep checking every 20 minutes and add a little more water to the pan if needed.

Leave to cool slightly, then pour into a sterilised glass jar and store in the fridge for up to a month.

PICO DE GALLO SALSA
Serves 4–6

This makes a good topping to serve with chicken fajitas (see page 142).

2 large ripe tomatoes, deseeded and cut into 5mm dice
½ onion, chopped
Handful of fresh coriander, chopped
1 green serrano or jalapeño chilli, finely chopped
¼ tsp salt
1 lime

Mix all the ingredients in a bowl, starting with the juice of half the lime and adding more to taste, if desired. Serve immediately.

PICKLED TURNIP
Makes a 1-litre jar

Nice with the falafel on page 100.

500g white turnips
150g beetroots

Pickling liquid
1½ tsp salt
1 tbsp sugar
250ml white wine vinegar
1 tsp coriander seeds
1 red chilli, sliced, seeds in

You will need a 1-litre sterilised Kilner-type jar. Peel the turnips and beetroots, cut them into batons 1cm thick, then pack them into the jar.

Pour 250ml of water into a pan and bring to the boil. Add the salt and sugar and stir until dissolved, then add the vinegar, coriander seeds and chilli. Pour the pickling liquid into the jar over the vegetables and seal. Ideally, store for a few weeks before using.

PICCALILLI

Makes about 6 x 450g jars

For me, this is a must to serve with scotch eggs (see page 40).

225g salt
2.5 litres hot water
1 medium cauliflower, broken into florets
225g pickling onions, peeled and halved
225g runner beans
½ large cucumber
100g caster sugar
1 garlic clove, crushed
900ml distilled malt vinegar, plus 2½ tbsp
¼ tsp ground allspice
¼ tsp freshly grated nutmeg
25g plain flour
2 tbsp English mustard powder
2 tbsp ground turmeric
1 tbsp ground ginger

You will need 6 x 450g sterilised jars
    with vinegar-proof lids.

Mix the 225g of salt with the hot water. Divide this between 2 large bowls and leave to cool.

Put the cauliflower and onions into one of the bowls of salt water. Top and tail the runner beans and cut them into 2.5cm pieces and put them in the other bowl. Cut the cucumber in half lengthways, scoop out the seeds, then cut the flesh into chunks and add them to the bowl with the beans. Put plates on top of the vegetables to keep them submerged and leave for 24 hours.

Drain the vegetables and rinse them well, keeping them separate. Put the sugar, garlic and 900ml of malt vinegar into a large stainless steel saucepan. Bring to the boil, then add the cauliflower, onions, allspice and nutmeg and cook for 3 minutes.

Add the runner beans and cucumber and cook for a further 4–5 minutes. The vegetables should be only just cooked, with a little crunch left in them. Lift them out of the pan with a slotted spoon and place in a large bowl. Set the pan of cooking liquid aside.

Mix the flour, mustard powder, turmeric and ground ginger with the 2½ tablespoons of distilled malt vinegar and enough water to make a smooth paste. Add a little of the hot vinegar mixture to the paste, stir the paste back into the pan of cooking liquid and bring to the boil, stirring. Simmer for 5 minutes, then stir the sauce into the vegetables.

Spoon the piccalilli into warm, sterilised jars, seal with vinegar-proof lids and leave to cool. The pickle is ready to eat immediately and will keep for up to a year.

POURING CUSTARD
Serves 4–6

A must-have with apple pie (see page 245).

1 vanilla pod
600ml whole milk
4 egg yolks
3 tbsp caster sugar
4 tsp cornflour

Slit open the vanilla pod and scrape out the seeds with the tip of a sharp knife. Put the milk, vanilla pod and seeds into a non-stick pan and bring to the boil. Remove the pan from the heat and set aside for 20 minutes or so to allow the flavour of vanilla to infuse the milk.

Beat the egg yolks, sugar and cornflour together in a bowl until smooth. Bring the milk back to the boil, remove the vanilla pod, then gradually beat the milk into the egg yolk mixture. Return the custard to the pan and cook over a medium heat, stirring constantly, until it thickens. Don't let it boil.

CRÈME CHANTILLY
Serves 4–6

Nice with strawberry sorbet (see page 236) or in a knickerbocker glory (see page 248).

150ml double or whipping cream
1 heaped tsp icing sugar, sifted
½ tsp vanilla paste or seeds scraped from a vanilla pod

Whisk the cream, sugar and vanilla paste or seeds in a bowl until thickened and holding soft peaks. Take care not to overwhip. Refrigerate until ready to use.

CLARIFIED BUTTER

Use in Indian cookery instead of ghee.

Place some butter in a small pan and leave it over a low heat until it has melted. Then skim off any scum from the surface and pour off the clear (clarified) butter into a bowl, leaving behind the milky white solids that will have settled on the bottom of the pan.

RICK'S PEPPERMIX
Makes a small jar

Good for the chicken burrito on page 136.

1 dried chipotle chilli, seeds removed
1 dried pasilla chilli, seeds removed
2 tbsp black peppercorns
2 tbsp white peppercorns
2 tsp Szechuan peppercorns
1 tbsp salt

Mix all the ingredients in a spice grinder and store in a jam jar until required.

GARAM MASALA
Makes 50g

This is my own garam masala recipe, which is essentially a balanced combination of the most popular spices. Even more important than the mix is having the spices freshly roasted and ground. I can't stress too strongly how much better it is to make your own garam masala than to buy it. You may be surprised at the number of times garam masala turns up in the book. But this mixture represents perfect balance to me, and the reason it appears so often is because once you've made it, it's easy to knock up a large number of recipes without resorting to teaspoons of this and that. I would recommend renewing the mixture every month.

1 tbsp black peppercorns
2 tbsp cumin seeds
2 tbsp coriander seeds
2 tsp cardamom seeds (from 30–40 green pods)
4 tsp whole cloves
7cm cinnamon stick
1 whole nutmeg

Roast all the spices, apart from the nutmeg, in a dry frying pan over a medium heat for a couple of minutes until toasted and aromatic, then leave to cool.

Grate the nutmeg and add it to a spice grinder along with the whole spices (you might want to break up the cinnamon stick) and grind everything to a fine powder.

Store in a sealed container out of the sunlight; the mixture will stay in its most aromatic condition for a month.

MASSAMAN CURRY PASTE
Makes enough for 2 curries

Use this for the Massaman beef curry on page 206. Keeps in the fridge for about two weeks.

10 dried red Kashmiri chillies,
    deseeded and roughly chopped
2 tbsp coriander seeds
1 tbsp cumin seeds
1 tsp cardamom seeds
    (from about 20 green pods)
16 cloves
5cm cinnamon stick
2 blades of mace
3 tbsp vegetable oil
200g shallots or onions, roughly chopped
25g garlic, peeled and roughly chopped
1 tsp Thai shrimp paste
25g root ginger, peeled and roughly chopped
2 fat lemongrass stalks, chopped
8 tbsp coconut milk

Put the chillies, with the coriander, cumin and cardamom seeds, cloves, cinnamon and mace in a dry frying pan. Fry for a minute or so until the spices smell fragrant but don't allow them to burn. Tip them into a spice grinder and grind to a fine powder.

Warm the oil in the pan and fry the shallots or onions and the garlic until soft but not browned. Add the shrimp paste and ground spices, then fry for 2–3 minutes. Tip everything back into the spice grinder or a blender or small food processor, add the ginger, lemongrass and coconut milk and blend to a fairly smooth paste.

Store the paste in a glass jar in the fridge until ready to use.

VEGETABLE STOCK
Makes about 2 litres

A good veg stock can make a great difference to a vegetarian soup.

2 large onions
2 large carrots
1 fennel bulb
2 celery sticks
1 garlic bulb
3 bay leaves
A few parsley stalks
1 tsp salt

Wash and roughly chop the vegetables – no need to peel the garlic. Put them in a large pan with the herbs and salt and add 3 litres of water. Bring to the boil and simmer for 45–60 minutes, then strain the stock through a fine sieve into a clean pan or bowl.

FISH STOCK
Makes about 1 litre

Use any fish except oily ones like mackerel, sardines, herrings, salmon and tuna. Lemon sole, brill and plaice are all good.

1kg fish bones and heads
1 onion, chopped
1 leek, washed and sliced
1 fennel bulb, sliced
100g celery, sliced
1 thyme sprig
30ml sunflower oil
100ml white wine

Chop the fish bones into 5–6cm pieces and put them in a large pan. Add the vegetables, thyme and oil. Put a lid on the pan, place it over a medium heat and cook everything gently for 5 minutes, not allowing it to colour. Add the white wine and 2.25 litres of water and bring the liquid just to the boil, then turn the heat down and simmer very gently for 20 minutes.

Strain the stock through a sieve and use as required. If not using immediately, leave to cool, then chill and refrigerate or freeze.

CHICKEN STOCK
Makes 1.5 litres

You can also use a leftover carcass and bones from a roast chicken to make this stock.

Bones from 1.5kg uncooked chicken
   or 500g chicken wings
1 large carrot, roughly chopped
2 celery sticks, roughly sliced
2 leeks, washed and sliced
2 fresh or dried bay leaves
2 thyme sprigs

Put all the ingredients into a large pan with 2.5 litres of water and bring to the boil. Skim off any scum that rises to the surface. Leave to simmer gently for about 2 hours – don't let it boil as an emulsion will form and make the stock cloudy.

Strain the stock through a fine sieve and use as required. If not using immediately, leave to cool, then chill and refrigerate or freeze. Or simmer the strained stock to reduce further and concentrate the flavour before storing.

BEEF STOCK
Makes about 2.4 litres

Good beef stock adds delicious flavour to dishes such as the beef and Guinness pie on page 203.

2 celery sticks, roughly chopped
2 carrots, roughly chopped
2 onions, roughly chopped
900g beef shin
2 bay leaves
2 thyme sprigs
1 tbsp salt
2 tbsp vegetable oil (if making a rich brown stock)

For a pale brown stock, put the vegetables and beef into a large pan with 5 litres of water and bring to the boil. Skim off any scum that rises to the surface. Simmer for 2½ hours, adding the herbs and salt for the last 15 minutes. Strain the stock through a fine sieve into a clean pan.

The stock is now ready to use, or can be chilled in the fridge or frozen for later use. You can also continue to cook it to reduce the liquid and make a richer stock.

For a richer-tasting brown beef stock, start by heating 2 tablespoons of vegetable oil in the pan. Add the vegetables and beef and fry them for 10–15 minutes until nicely browned. Then add the water and cook as above, adding the herbs and salt 15 minutes before the end of cooking.

CONVERSIONS

MEASUREMENTS

METRIC	IMPERIAL
5mm	¼in
1.25cm	½ in
2.5cm	1in
5cm	2in
7.5cm	3in
10cm	4in
12.5cm	5in
15cm	6in
18cm	7in
20cm	8in
23cm	9in
25cm	10in
30cm	12in

VOLUME

METRIC	IMPERIAL
25ml	1fl oz
50ml	2fl oz
85ml	3fl oz
100ml	3½fl oz
150ml	5fl oz
200ml	7fl oz
300ml	10fl oz
450ml	15fl oz
600ml	1 pint
700ml	1¼ pints
900ml	1½ pints
1 litre	1¾ pints
1.2 litres	2 pints
1.25 litres	2¼ pints
1.5 litres	2½ pints
1.6 litres	2¾ pints
1.75 litres	3 pints
2 litres	3½ pints
2.25 litres	4 pints
2.75 litres	5 pints
3.4 litres	6 pints
3.9 litres	7 pints
4.5 litres	8 pints (1 gallon)

WEIGHTS

METRIC	IMPERIAL
15g	½oz
25g	1oz
40g	1½oz
50g	2oz
75g	3oz
100g	4oz
150g	5oz
175g	6oz
200g	7oz
225g	8oz
250g	9oz
275g	10oz
350g	12oz
375g	13oz
400g	14oz
425g	15oz
450g	1lb
550g	1¼lb
675g	1½lb
750g	1¾lb
900g	2lb
1.5kg	3lb
1.75kg	4lb
2.25kg	5lb

OVEN TEMPERATURES

°C	°C FAN	°F	GAS
110	90	225	¼
120	100	250	½
140	120	275	1
150	130	300	2
160	140	325	3
180	160	350	4
190	170	375	5
200	180	400	6
220	200	425	7
230	210	450	8
240	220	475	9

COOK'S NOTES

Generally, I don't specify the weight of garlic cloves, tomatoes, carrots or onions because the reality of cooking is that you just take a clove or two of garlic or a whole onion or a handful of herbs. However, in case it's helpful, I thought it would be sensible to suggest the weights I have in mind.

1 garlic clove: 5g
1 small onion (unpeeled): 100g
1 medium onion (unpeeled): 175g
1 large onion (unpeeled): 225g
Small handful of fresh herbs: about 15g
Large handful of fresh herbs: about 30g
Large pinch of spice: about ⅛ tsp

All teaspoon and tablespoon measurements are level unless otherwise stated and are based on measuring spoons:

1 teaspoon: 5ml
1 tablespoon: 15ml
Readers in Australia will need to make minor adjustments, as their tablespoon measure is 20ml.

EGGS AND CHICKEN
Use medium free-range eggs in the recipes, unless otherwise specified. And use free-range chicken if possible.

TEMPERATURE PROBE
The most accurate way of assessing whether meat is cooked correctly is to use a temperature probe. This is a cheap gadget and you get far more accurate results than by relying on cooking times alone. Use your calculated time as a guide, then test the internal temperature against the table below. Insert the probe into the thickest part of the meat, not too close to the bone, and leave it for at least 10 seconds.

Always bring meat and poultry up to room temperature before cooking. Bear in mind that meat and fish continue to cook after being removed from the heat; their temperature rises by about 6°C. Meat and poultry benefit from resting after being cooked and before serving.

47–50°C very rare
50–52°C rare
55–57°C medium rare
60–62°C medium
65–67°C medium well done
71+°C well done

INDEX

ACKNOWLEDGEMENTS

I would like to thank everyone at Ebury Publishing for what is a great team but particularly Joel Rickett, managing director; Albert DePetrillo, publishing director; editors, Nell Warner and Katie Fisher; and my long-term publicist, Claire Scott.

I've come to realise that the success of every book I do is completely dependent on everyone who works with me. When I wrote my first book *English Seafood Cookery* in 2001, I did virtually everything myself, including employing a freelance publicist to get me on to various television programmes and into newspapers. Now, the team effort is everything and I find that one of the most important parts of writing a book is working with other people. As I write these acknowledgements I feel a bit like Van Morrison, who I saw in concert recently – he thanked the individual members of the band and, as he did so, they each played a little riff.

So, here goes with my band: on lead guitar, Portia Spooner who's contributed so much to these recipes. On bass, project editor Jinny Johnson – the bass is always in the background, but you sure do miss them when they're not there. Photographer James Murphy and designers Alex and Emma Smith – my brass section bringing lots of rousing colour and skill. And on rhythm guitars, food stylist Jan Smith and prop stylist Penny Markham, adding those notes of perfection. Then you can't do without percussion – photography assistants Toby Woollen and Lucia Lowther, food styling assistant Nicola Roberts, proofreader Elise See Tai and indexer Hilary Bird.

Viv Taylor, my PA of 23 years' standing, is on drums, keeping everything on time. Then naturally there is the soloist – my dear wife Sas, always looking marvellous and the best support.

I'm also happy to be thanking the TV crew on *Food Stories* in conjunction with the book. It hasn't happened for the last few years, but they have been so important for this one. Thanks to Matt Bennett, executive producer and director for Shine TV; Cazzie Topliss, producer; Colin Steele, second director; Julie Gilmartin, production manager; Chris Topliss, first cameraman; Martin Willcocks, second cameraman; Pete Underwood, sound recordist and everyone's confidant – loves to think of himself as second director; Will Spooner, Portia's son, running duties and driving.

Many thanks to Shepherd's Bush Market and their community manager, Alecia.

I would also like to thank the following for sharing their recipes with me: Pam Brunton, Bundobust, Nallaine Calvo, Rachel Green, Gullus Kitchen, Mark Hix, Nicola Hordern, Gaz Oakley, Kimberley Prado, Helen Rebanks, Mitch Turner, Yoven Virasami.

Finally, I would like acknowledge the following, whose words or work I have mentioned: Anthony Burgess, Robert Frost, Barclay James Harvest, Robert Herrick, Paul McCartney, Jennifer Stead and Warren Zevon.

The recipe for Herdwick Mutton Hotpot on page 170 (copyright © Helen Rebanks 2023) is reproduced by permission of United Agents Ltd on behalf of Helen Rebanks.

BBC Books, an imprint of Ebury Publishing
One Embassy Gardens, 8 Viaduct Gdns, Nine Elms, London SW11 7BW

BBC Books is part of the Penguin Random House
group of companies whose addresses can be found
at global.penguinrandomhouse.com

Penguin
Random House
UK

This book is published to accompany the television series entitled *Rick Stein's Food Stories*
first broadcast on BBC Two in 2024. *Rick Stein's Food Stories* is a Shine production.

Producer: Cazzie Topliss
Director: Colin Steele
Executive Producer and Director: Matt Bennett
BBC Commissioning Editor: Rachel Platt

First published by BBC Books in 2024
www.penguin.co.uk

A CIP catalogue record for this book is available from the British Library

ISBN 9781785948602

Commissioning editor: Albert DePetrillo
Editors: Nell Warner and Katie Fisher
Project editor: Jinny Johnson
Design: Smith & Gilmour
Photography: James Murphy
Photography assistants: Toby Woollen and Lucia Lowther
Food stylist: Jan Smith
Food styling assistant: Nicola Roberts
Prop stylist: Penny Markham
Proofreader: Elise See Tai
Indexer: Hilary Bird

Printed and bound in Germany by Mohn Media GmbH
Colour origination by Altaimage, London

The authorised representative in the EEA is Penguin Random House Ireland,
Morrison Chambers, 32 Nassau Street, Dublin D02 YH68.

Penguin Random House is committed to a sustainable future for our business, our readers
and our planet. This book is made from Forest Stewardship Council® certified paper.